More Acclaim for *A Woman in the House*

"*A Woman in the House* is the story of a true leader, former member of Congress Pat Saiki, a woman whose leadership has made a difference in the lives of so many—inspiring small business women and men, helping families and educating children. It is a book that gives us the secret to true and lasting success and one that should be provided to every young person seeking to find their way in life. Among the many important lessons in the book: Pat Saiki built her career on a foundation of service, and her story provides important insights about how to persevere in the face of great obstacles."

—Patricia Harrison, president and CEO,
Corporation for Public Broadcasting

"It was Pat Saiki who encouraged me to seriously consider running for Congress. When I decided to run, I did so inspired by Pat's record of accomplishments at the state and national levels. Thank you, Pat, for many years of public service, and for being a guiding light for so many women in Hawaii and across our great country."

—U.S. Senator Susan Collins (R-Maine),
Washington, D.C.

"Kazuo and Shizue Fukuda, Pat Saiki's hardworking parents, laid the foundation for her remarkable life. They always encouraged her to strive to be the best, and were always there to support her, her husband, Dr. Stanley Saiki, and their five children. Those lessons left their mark; their daughter eventually shaped public policy as a state lawmaker in Hawaii, played key roles in Congress approving reparations for Japanese Americans interned in World War II, ended the U.S. Navy's bombing of Kahoolawe, and counseled presidents of both Hawaii's largest corporations and the United States."

—Franklin Kometani, DDS,
former Saiki campaign chairman

"We have a lot to learn from Pat Saiki's life. It has been full, and she has always done it her way! Never one to mince words and always a force to be reckoned with, Pat was a pioneer in fighting establishments, promoting women's rights, and championing individual freedom and choice. A committed believer in a two-party system, she knew how to work across the aisle to get stuff done, a rare and precious talent in today's partisan political world."

—*Dr. Charles Morrison,*
former president, East-West Center

"Pat Saiki paved the way for women like me who wanted to make a positive difference in people's lives. Her ability to affect positive change through groundbreaking legislation while navigating a tough political environment illustrates her special gift for public service. Pat and I are from different generations, so I did not have a chance to serve with her, but because of her many legislative successes and real-life example of servant leadership, I was able to be elected as a Republican mayor of Maui County and governor of Hawaii in an overwhelmingly Democrat state. I am indebted to her and grateful for all she did for the people of Hawaii."

—*Linda Lingle,*
governor of Hawaii, 2002–10

a Woman in the House

PAT SAIKI

WATERMARK
PUBLISHING

ISBN 978-1-948011-52-5

Library of Congress Control Number: 2021932802

Photo credits
Interior and back cover photos courtesy of the author, front cover photo and p. 90 *Honolulu Star-Advertiser*, front cover illustration iStock/alexkava, pp. 128 and 129 Floyd K. Takeuchi

Design and production
Ingrid Lynch

Watermark Publishing
1000 Bishop St., Ste. 806
Honolulu, HI 96813
Toll-free 1-866-900-BOOK
sales@bookshawaii.net
www.bookshawaii.net

10 9 8 7 6 5 4 3 2 1

Printed in Korea

Contents

Introduction

I got to know Pat Saiki well when she first ran for the U.S. House of Representatives in 1986. I was a political reporter in those days. Those of us who were covering the race quickly figured out that Pat was one of the most accomplished campaigners we'd ever seen. She had an uncanny knack for asking a question then finding some connection with the astonished voter.

Pat cruised to victory, which was a shock to many in a state that until that election had never put a Republican in one of Hawaii's two seats in the U.S. House of Representatives.

About a week after the election, I interviewed Pat for a postelection analysis story. After the interview, she asked if I'd join her Washington staff as press secretary, a wonderful, old-fashioned title still in use at that time. It didn't take long to say yes. I admired Pat's fighting spirit—she was unafraid of fighting the good fight—but she knew that governing was about more than political one-upmanship.

I also admired Pat's core belief that she was elected to make government serve the people, not to serve as a litmus test for political purity. I saw that play out in Congress. As had been the case in the Hawaii state legislature, where Pat rang up a series of major legislative accomplishments by working with the majority Democrats and often letting them claim credit, Pat played a key role in passing legislation that righted an historic wrong.

A bill to apologize and offer reparations for the internment of Japanese Americans during World War II was stuck in the U.S. House of Representatives. There were enough Republican "no" votes to hold up passage of the bill. Pat eagerly took on the task of working her caucus, one member at a time, explaining why she backed the bill, and asking for their support. Despite being a lowly freshman, Pat spoke with unusual authority in the caucus. Not only was she obviously Japanese American, she was the first from her party to represent Hawaii in the House of Representatives. (Senator Hiram Fong, a Republican, was the first Asian American to serve in the U.S. Senate and had served in Congress since statehood.)

After years of inaction, Pat's efforts turned enough Republican votes in the House to ensure passage of the reparations bill.

Pat's stubborn determination probably explains much of her success. She'll stick with it and won't let the "lolos" (*lolo* is Hawaiian for "feeble-minded") on the other side get away with an easy victory. If Pat is anything, it is determined.

But I think there's another reason for Pat's remarkable record of success in the public arena, and in life. She is her father's daughter. Her memoir begins with a nod to her father, Kazuo Fukuda, a quiet, dignified man who instilled in his three daughters the importance of respect, sacrifice and—by teaching them to play competitive tennis—the drive and will to win.

"Mr. Fukuda," as Pat's staff called him with much affection, worked as a clerk at American Factors (Amfac), one of Hawaii's "Big Five" corporations that dominated political, economic and social life in the Islands for generations. Decades later, his oldest daughter, Patricia, by then a prominent member of the Hawaii Legislature, was invited to serve as a director of Amfac. Before she accepted the historic honor (she was the first woman to be asked to serve on the board of a major Hawaii company) Pat asked her father for his advice and approval.

She didn't have to do that, of course. But Pat knew instinctively that by asking her father, he would know he'd won his long, difficult battle to leave his children a more equitable world. Pat would also be able to say to him, "Pops, we did it." And she kept on doing it, from the state legislature to the U.S. Congress to the Cabinet Room in the White House.

—Floyd K. Takeuchi

Pat Saiki's father taught her to play tennis, and she was a competitive player.

PART I

The Early Years
1930–1968

Hopes and Expectations

I was born on May 28, 1930, in Hilo, a bustling business community on the northeastern side of the Big Island of Hawaii, the first of three daughters my parents, Kazuo and Shizue Fukuda, would have over the next eight years.[1] My father must surely have wished for a son, but every time he turned around, there was another girl. It didn't matter. He was a happy man who had enormous pride in his daughters. He affectionately called each of us "sonny boy," encouraged us to play competitive sports and voiced the same hopes and expectations for us that he would for any son. I like to call him "the original feminist."

My mother and father were second-generation Japanese Americans whose parents were recruited from Japan in the late 1890s to work the cane fields for Hilo Sugar Company. My father's family came from Kumamoto, on the Japanese island of Kyushu; my mother's from Hiroshima, the Honshu island city whose residents would suffer unprecedented devastation and loss when the U.S. dropped the atomic bomb during World War II.

Like tens of thousands of other early immigrants, my grandparents, Matsuzo and Yusu Fukuda, were brought in to plant, cultivate and harvest sugarcane at a time when worldwide demand for Hawaiian sugar far exceeded the island's supply of laborers.[2] As tenant farmers, my paternal grandparents worked their own plot of land and paid their rent by giving a portion of each year's harvest to the Hilo Sugar Company. The system kept overhead costs low for the company, which also recruited paid laborers from the local community, along with immigrants from Portugal, China and South Pacific islands. At the height of its production, the sugar mill processed 1,400 tons of sugar daily.[3]

Most of the Japanese cane field workers lived in an area known as "Japanese Camp." They stuck together and helped each other. When someone needed to build a home, neighbors pitched in to offer their skills as carpenters, electricians, plumbers and painters. Others leveled ground for foundations or prepared food for workers.[4] Families celebrated together—every marriage, birth, graduation or anniversary—and took care of each other.

Younger men in the community would turn out to chop wood for elderly men and widows. And when none of Hawaii's banks would lend money to these "aliens," they created a fund to help each other in case of emergencies or financial need. This loosely organized *kumiai* (community group, or union) allowed them to pool money in a fund they called *tanomoshi*. The *kumiai* would evaluate a family's needs and issue loans at nearly no interest. Because everyone was invested in the process, the *kumiai* kept the community together in mutual trust and confidence.

My grandparents worked hard and believed in education as the path to greater opportunity and freedom. My Fukuda grandparents sent their eldest son to college on the mainland U.S., where he earned a degree as a certified public accountant. The expectation was that he would return to Hilo, where the entire family would benefit from his higher status and earning potential as a college-educated professional.

It was not to be. Within a few years of returning home, he died of a fast-growing cancer. My father was second in line, but with no more funding available he had no opportunity to pursue higher education. He went to work as a clerk in the Hilo office of Amfac, a land-development company founded in Hawaii in 1849 as a retail and sugar business. It was his first job, and the one he would have his entire career.

My mother worked as a sales clerk at the Ah Mai[5] dry goods store in Hilo. She was also a talented seamstress, with many loyal clients. A steady stream of people came through our home for fittings in the small bedroom she used as her shop. My mother was particularly gifted at designing original fashions and drafting her own patterns. She sold custom dresses for $14, a small fortune in those days.

The sense of obligation and respect my parents had for their own parents was obvious and made a clear impression. It is an old Japanese tradition to observe rituals of respect toward one's elders. One of the rituals my father emphasized was making regular visits to see his parents. Every Saturday afternoon, he led the climb up Ponohawai Hill to their home. The path took us through cane fields, where we'd often see our uncle, my father's youngest brother, out working the family plot.

My grandparents lived in a raised home, built on stilts to protect it from flooding during frequent rains. My sisters and I loved poking around in the area under their home, creating a play space from this area used mostly for storage.

Meals were cooked inside, over an open fire. I've never tasted better rice than what my grandparents cooked in their big kettles. The toilet was outside, as was the *furo*, a Japanese-style, stand-alone wooden tub. Bathing in the *furo* required a preliminary scrubdown with soap and water and a thorough rinse. Clean water for the *furo* was heated over a fire.

My grandparents were steeped in Japanese tradition. I remember my grandmother's disapproval when she saw me wearing shorts, which she didn't consider suitably feminine. She frowned when I scrambled up trees to pick mountain apples and mangoes, but always enjoyed eating the fruits I harvested.

One of my most enjoyable childhood activities was also one of the most dangerous. In the early years, sugarcane was harvested by hand. Spear-sharp cuttings were lashed together into bundles and placed into flumes of rushing water to travel long distances to the mill.[6] The children of Hilo couldn't resist the temptation of catching a thrilling ride as those bundles made their way down the flumes.

Lunas—*luna* is the Hawaiian word for "supervisor"—were assigned to monitor the process and make sure the bundled cane stayed within the flumes. The lunas, mostly Portuguese immigrants, patrolled the fields on horseback. They sternly pulled children away from the flumes, partly to protect their safety, partly to protect the company from liability in case of an accident. But the lunas couldn't be everywhere at once, and when they were absent, adventurous kids would climb up to ride those lethal bundles.

I was fortunate; I never fell off a bundle while riding the flumes. But I shudder to think of the risks we took to have fun. A fall could mean a catastrophic and possibly deadly spearing by the swiftly moving, sharp-ended bundles of freshly cut cane.

A Tradition of Respect for Education

Both of my parents worked hard, saving as much of their income as they could to prepare for the higher education opportunities they wanted all of their children to have. My father walked to work every day to avoid the expense of a car. My mother, despite her steady work as a seamstress, somehow made time to sew the clothing needed by three rapidly growing daughters.

My parents, in the tradition of their own parents, valued learning above all else. We girls grew up imbued with a sense of respect for knowledge and those who teach. Some of the manifestations of that attitude may seem a bit extreme given today's standards, but they left a profound impression. One example: You never, ever sat on a pile of books to raise yourself higher on a chair. Books were considered sacred; to use them for anything but reading was disrespecting the wise minds of the people who wrote them.

Hilo pre-statehood offered two types of schools at the elementary level. A child's placement in either was considered very important. We took tests to determine whether we would pursue our education in a traditional public school or enter what was called a "standard" school. Standard schools offered more advanced coursework, similar to what today's accelerated, or "gifted" programs might provide. We all took the tests. Only those who qualified were accepted into Hilo Standard School. In retrospect, it was a terribly discriminatory process. Fortunately, this practice—heavily weighted in favor of children who spoke in "proper" rather than "pidgin" English—did not last long.

I was just a child, so I didn't really think about it one way or another. I took the tests, did my best and followed along with whatever my parents and teachers encouraged me to do. I easily passed the exams and enrolled in Hilo Standard School. I never felt that I was special, but I remember people speaking of me as though I were predetermined to succeed: "After all, she qualified for Hilo Standard School." But as I matured, my mind echoed with reminders of that early discrimination, and I wondered how this system affected the morale and self-esteem of my Hilo Union peers. We all met up again in seventh grade at Hilo Intermediate, which funneled us all into Hilo High School.

I liked school and worked hard to earn good grades. I never felt any pressure to be at the top of my class but always felt I belonged in the top two or three. I particularly enjoyed Latin classes with Mr. Putman, a crusty old guy who nevertheless endeared himself to me and provided me with a meaningful foundation in the language.

I embraced opportunities for leadership, always feeling that I had a knack for organization. I successfully ran for class officer and particularly enjoyed my role as president of the high school tennis club.

My father was an athletic soul whose favorite sport was tennis. As soon as I could hold a racquet, he was teaching me how to stroke, volley and serve. His skills were well known and respected in our community; everyone wanted him as their coach. Eventually, he took a position coaching the Hilo High School tennis club, an independent program not sponsored by the school. He was also the volunteer tennis coach at St. Joseph School in Hilo. My father loved coaching and the respect and status it conveyed. My role as tennis club president gave us wonderful opportunities to share our passion for the sport. He traveled with the team when we competed with Honokaa, Laupahoehoe and other high schools on the island.

Thanks in great part to his effective coaching, I became quite adept at the sport and competed territory-wide.[7]

I cherished one-on-one time with my father. Sometimes, when I walked home from school, I'd stop at his office and he'd take me across the street to the drug store for ice cream sodas and conversation. My father constantly reminded me that girls could be successful in sports—and in any career we might choose. His voice remains clear and strong in my memory: "You can be anything you want to be and do anything you choose to pursue. Being a girl should not hinder you in any way. That is, of course, if you study hard, go to college and find a job—maybe as a school teacher, a nurse or even a lawyer."

Then he would go back to work and I would walk the rest of the way home.

The Fallout of War

Our comfortable rural life was threatened when Japan attacked Pearl Harbor on December 7, 1941, and the United States entered World War II. All island residents felt their lives were at risk, but those of us of Japanese descent—especially those considered aliens in the U.S. territory because they lacked U.S. citizenship—came under intense scrutiny.

My family built a bomb shelter in our backyard and buried anything overtly Japanese, including dishes, books and clothes. We had to blacken the windows, abide by strict curfews and respect martial law.

In March 1942, President Franklin D. Roosevelt signed Executive Order 9066, authorizing the removal of any or all people from military areas "as deemed necessary or desirable."[8] By June, more than 110,000 Japanese Americans, most from the West Coast, were relocated to one of ten remote internment camps in scattered locations around the country.

In Hawaii, the Japanese American population was too prevalent, and too important to the local economy, to be rounded up in total, so only the leaders of the community were detained.[9] We were sickened when honorable people who were journalists, businessmen, teachers of the Japanese language and leaders of community organizations were herded into internment camps without due process. We were not "dangerous Japs." We were ordinary residents suffering from the trauma of the Pearl Harbor attack, just like anyone else on the islands.

My uncle Shingo Narikawa, my mother's brother-in-law, was one of the businessmen rounded up with other Hawaii residents suspected of disloyalty. At first, they were imprisoned at local jails. When the U.S. Army opened Honouliuli Internment Camp on Oahu in 1943,[10] my uncle was confined there—along with 400 other Japanese-, German- and Italian American internees and 4,000 prisoners of war.[11] They called the camp Jigoku-Dani, or "Hell's Valley," because of its secluded location in a hot, humid and mosquito-infested gulch.[12] Anyone hoping to visit a family member confined to the camp had to be blindfolded and bused from Honolulu to the camp, which was surrounded by agricultural fields not far from Pearl Harbor.[13]

When Uncle Narikawa was told he would be moved to the Topaz War Relocation Center in Millard County, Utah, he was asked if he wanted his wife and children, who were U.S. citizens, to go with him. It's not likely they had a choice.

They were all shipped off to the camp, located about 140 miles southwest of Salt Lake City, in a dry, windy environment with harsh winters that must have come as quite a shock to a family from the temperate, tropical Hawaiian Islands. Even today, I call my cousin "Topaz" Narikawa, because he and his family were forced to live in the camp until the end of the war in 1945.

Uncle Narikawa had the good sense to give my father, who was a U.S. citizen, his power of attorney. That kept his business and family holdings safe until the end of the war. Few, if any, records were kept of this time in my family history. I am not aware of any letters or photos from family members who were imprisoned. Like most Japanese families affected, my relatives stoically accepted their lot, despite the humiliation of being rounded up like criminals and the discomfort of living in barn-like conditions. But this unbelievable, illegal treatment of law-abiding aliens and Americans of Japanese ancestry left a scar in my heart and I swore I would find a way to right this wrong. It would take nearly four decades to make good on that promise.

A Record-Setting Tsunami

Tsunamis aren't common in Hawaii, but when they occur anywhere on an arc from north in the Aleutian Islands to the west coast of South America, Hilo Bay on the Big Island is often most affected. Hilo's underwater bayfront acts like a funnel to amplify incoming waves, creating abnormal height and strong inland surges.[14]

At 6:54 a.m. on April Fools' Day 1946, an 8.6 magnitude earthquake off the Aleutians triggered the most destructive tsunami in modern Hawaiian history.[15] It hit with no warning, and by the time the wave receded, 159 people were dead. The wave that hit Hilo was three stories tall.

I was then 16 years old. When we heard a tsunami was coming, we all rushed outside to see it—we were curious! I remember watching the water from the first giant wave raging up Kumu Street just below our house, which was far enough inland to be safely out of reach. When the second wave came in, it was monstrous. We could hear the crunch and crackle of impact as water collided forcefully with homes and businesses. We could see huge swaths of debris floating in the street. The Amfac lumberyard was caught in the wave and lumber came rushing out, crashing and splintering along the way.

My grandmother on my mother's side (who was then already a widow), two of my mother's brothers and her disabled sister lived in Shinmachi, a small community located on low-lying land near Hilo's waterfront.[16] When the tsunami hit, water came right over the beach and slammed into Shinmachi. The people were caught between the ocean and a canal.

The only building strong enough to withstand the waves was owned by the Coca-Cola Bottling Company. My mother's brother, Uncle Rango Inoue, climbed to the building's rooftop and yelled to everyone he could see, urging them to come into the building. He knew it was their only chance to escape being swept into the canal along with the ruins of their community. Many people survived because of his bravery.

Soon after the waves and the initial shock of the event subsided, my mother decided she and my father should go to Shinmachi to see what had happened to Grandma Inoue and the rest of the family. They walked across ramps leading up to the Coca-Cola building, frightened and horrified as they saw bodies below them on both sides of the ramp. But they did find their family. Everyone was safe.

The tsunami essentially swept Shinmachi off the map.[17] The community was painstakingly rebuilt, without any financial support from the U.S., likely because of continuing anti-Japanese sentiment. Mainland press coverage of the tsunami avoided mentioning Shinmachi altogether, focusing only on the casualties to white people.[18]

Even today, those who had relatives in Shinmachi recall the horrors of that day. The stunning loss of life and property prompted creation of a territory-wide tsunami warning system.[19] The Seismic Sea Wave Warning System was established on August 12, 1948, and was later named the Pacific Tsunami Warning System.[20]

Despite the warning system, Shinmachi was completely destroyed again in 1960, when an 8.6 magnitude earthquake off the coast of

South Central Chile triggered a tsunami. The vulnerable Shinmachi site was never rebuilt and is now part of the Wailoa State Park.

From Student to Beauty Queen to Teacher

Despite the trauma of war and devastation from the tsunami, life—and work—went on. Our community adjusted to the new reality, rebuilding, coming to terms with anxiety and loss and focusing on hopes for a brighter future.

In 1948, I graduated from Hilo High School and gained admission to the University of Hawaii on the island of Oahu. It was the university's only campus in those days. That meant leaving home, boarding an airplane for the first time and understanding that there was no return date in sight. I respected the family budget constraints and understood I could not expect the luxury of traveling back and forth to Hilo for holiday visits.

My mother's brother, Uncle Yoichi Inoue, and his wife welcomed me into their Oahu home until I could transfer to campus housing. Aunty Dot was Korean, which created something of a scandal in the family when they first married. (It was traditional, and expected, that Japanese marry their own kind.) It didn't take long for Aunty Dot to win everyone over.

After a few months, I moved into Hale Laulima ("House of Cooperation"), a women-only dormitory just off the main campus, where each of us took responsibility for cooking, cleaning and serving food. After a year, I felt the pull to find a job and earn my own way. I wanted my parents to be able to shift financial resources to my sister June, who was just two years behind me.

Luck was on my side when my dormmates suggested I enter the contest to become a Kapalapala Beauty Queen. Then the only ethnically diverse beauty contest held at the University of Hawaii, the pageant offered attention that brought many opportunities to the winners.

I didn't think of myself as the beauty pageant type. For one thing, I didn't know how to walk like a pageant contestant. My friends showed me. I didn't know what to wear. My mother made a gown for me. We couldn't afford to fly me back to Hilo for a fitting, so she made the dress based on her recollection of my measurements, then sent it to Honolulu with hope that it would fit. And it did—perfectly.

The pageant itself was pretty simple. No swimsuit contest. No performance of a talent or skill. We simply had to walk across the stage in our beautiful gowns and await the judges' decisions. My parents were so sure I didn't have a chance they didn't even come to watch the event. They were just as surprised as I was to hear I'd won in the Japanese American category.

In 1946, the Chinese American businessman and publisher Ruddy Tongg[21] had created a new interisland airline called Trans-Pacific Airlines, which quickly became known as Aloha Airlines. (Tongg had several times been denied passage when trying to fly interisland on Hawaiian Airlines, so he decided to start one of his own to serve the needs of locals.) Soon after the Kapalapala pageant, Tongg came to the University of Hawaii seeking flight attendants to work part-time on weekends and holidays—and especially when Kilauea, one of the world's most active volcanoes, erupted on the Big Island, which in those days meant extra flights to meet the demand from thrill-seekers eager to see the dramatic event for themselves.

We pageant winners were offered employment. The job was perfect. We were paid well, earning double when the volcano was active because eruptions were unpredictable and we had to rush to the airport to go to work with little advance warning. My parents were not too happy about my flying over an erupting volcano, but with the typical nonchalance of youth, I never worried about my safety. I enjoyed working with my fellow contestant winners—Ruth Awai (later Mrs. Ruddy Tongg), Chinese queen; Ethel Jean Ho (later Kam), Korean queen; and Jackie Booth (later Benham), mixed-ethnicity "cosmopolitan" queen.

I also modeled clothes for the later-named Ritz department stores[22] in exchange for my wardrobe, and did some babysitting for extra money. I managed to meet my own expenses, which allowed my parents to support my sister June through college on the mainland.

It was never a question that I would help. I had seen what happened to my father—how his own hopes for a college education were dashed simply because he was the second son—and I felt responsible for becoming self-sufficient as quickly as possible so my sisters also would have opportunities to advance.

In my senior year at UH, I was offered a teaching job at the historic Punahou School, founded in 1841 on lands given to Christian missionaries by Hawaiian *alii* (chiefs).[23] It was then, as it is today, an exclusive private school for grades K–12. Until then, the school had only hired teachers from the mainland. The president at that time, John Fox, wanted Punahou to include local teachers on the faculty. I signed a contract on the spot, and after earning my bachelor of science degree, with a minor in education, I assumed my teaching position at Punahou in the fall of 1952.[24]

My decision to major in science was intentional. Though I wanted to have teaching as a career option, my feeling was that the UH College of Education at that time concentrated too much on the methods of teaching rather than creating experts who could teach specific subject matters. With a minor in education, and completion of the required certification steps with the state Department of Education, I could be hired as a teacher. The science degree made it possible for me to teach specific subject areas, which seemed so much more sensible. I swore that someday, if I could, I would push to modernize the curriculum at the College of Education.

At Punahou, I taught junior high physical education. I was known as the "local teacher in white shorts." I taught a wide range of sports to boys and girls, including swimming. My special pleasure was helping coordinate the annual Aquacade, a synchronized swimming event, with Roland "Rollie" Higgins, a fellow teacher and swimmer well known for his aquatic skills—and for developing that talent in his student athletes.[25] Those were the days when "aquamusicals" were popularized by actress/swimmer Esther Williams, who made a series of films in the 1940s and '50s. The Punahou Aquacade ran three nights in a row and was very popular with students. It attracted tremendous public support and many tickets were sold.

After about a year of teaching, I had earned enough money to do something I had always wanted to do: I bought a car for my father. For my entire childhood he had made the sacrifice to walk to work every day to save money for his daughters' education. I flew to Hilo one weekend to purchase a used car for him—a blue, four-door Dodge that had once been a taxi, so it was *very* well used! I made a second visit home to teach him how to drive it. I didn't have a car of my own, of course, but I dated boys who did. They taught me to drive so I could earn my driver's license.

Teaching my father to drive was quite the role-reversal experience for both of us. He was not used to his eldest daughter telling him what to do! Seeing his face behind the wheel was one of my greatest pleasures. Outwardly, he remained the stoic, Japanese gentleman, but I could see in his eyes just how delighted he was. With his own "wheels," he was a new man.

Wife, Mother, Teacher and Activist

After two years teaching at Punahou School, my life changed with the excitement of marriage to Dr. Stanley Mitsuo Saiki, a surgeon and general practitioner. I guess I should give credit to my Aunty Dot Inoue, who engineered the whole thing.

Dr. Saiki was Aunty Dot's physician. He was then in his early thirties and practicing medicine in partnership with his brother-in-law, Dr. Sam Tashima. They had an office in Kaimuki in Honolulu. Aunty Dot pestered me for weeks, telling me I needed to meet Dr. Saiki. I was not convinced. To me, the idea of dating a man 13 years my senior didn't sound like much fun. An older man's idea of a date is going out to dinner, I thought. Boring! But Aunty Dot was relentless.

One day, she said, "I'm putting my foot down. Go out with Dr. Saiki, or you can't do your laundry here on the weekends!" She must have pestered him, too, eventually threatening to find another doctor if he didn't ask me for a date. He relented, asked me out and guess what? We went to dinner.

I was surprised to find how much we had in common and how much I enjoyed his company. I was attracted to his calm, confident manner, his intelligence, his compassion for his patients and his devotion to his family.

Stanley grew up in Koloa, Kauai, with a brother and three sisters. He attended public schools and did exceptionally well. After graduating from Kauai High School, he spent two years at the University of Hawaii and then transferred as a junior to the University of North Dakota in Grand Forks, where his uncle served on the faculty.

Uncle Arthur Saiki, MD, was married to a Caucasian woman and they had two sons: George (we called him Buzzy) and John, who became a physician. Their mother died at an early age and Uncle Arthur sent the two boys to live on Kauai with Stanley's family. So the relationships among the boys, their father and Stanley were close. Dr. Saiki, a pathologist, was recognized as an outstanding physician and was called upon regularly by Mayo Clinic for his opinions. He was an inspiration to Stanley and undoubtedly influenced his decision to go into medicine.

After two years in Grand Forks—during which Stanley attended school while also working odd jobs to fund his education—he was accepted to medical school at Temple University in Philadelphia, one of the few programs that accepted students from territorial Hawaii without first requiring them to establish residency on the mainland. When he completed his medical training, he returned home to Honolulu to join his brother-in-law's practice.

Stanley and I dated for a few months and soon knew we were ready to make our relationship permanent. In proper "Japanese custom," as Stan said, he wanted to go to Hilo to meet my parents and explain his intentions. He played his part very well—he even played a round of golf with my father and let him win! My parents took to Stanley, as I knew they would. They were sold, and gave us their blessing.

In Honolulu, things were not so warm with his family. They

thought Stanley should marry a woman of standing in the Japanese community—someone who knew flower arranging, not tennis and golf. A ladylike *ojosan*, not a tomboy, would have been preferable to them. Rather than put up with this disapproval, we decided to arrange for a wedding in Los Angeles in early 1954. Stanley's medical school classmate, Dr. Gordon Salness, and his wife were more than willing to stand up for us and help us arrange a proper ceremony.

Stan's relatives who lived in Los Angeles attended the church service and reception. My parents sent their best regards. After the wedding, we left by train, bound for Detroit—my first cross-country adventure, which I found fascinating and exciting. We bought a car in Detroit and drove to Philadelphia so Stan could begin a one-year graduate medical program at the University of Pennsylvania School of Medicine.

We found an apartment in Roxborough, on the outskirts of Philadelphia, and set up our household. It was not long before I learned I was pregnant. An engaging couple from Germany lived in the apartment below us. They had a car, but the man didn't know how to drive, so I offered to teach him. We went on many practice drives in the neighborhood. He was a quick learner and appreciated the help. My husband, however, was not so enthusiastic. He was quite displeased that I would take unnecessary risks in my condition.

My rambunctious activities continued to irritate Stan. We had befriended my obstetrician/gynecologist, who owned a boat and invited us to go fishing with his family on a nearby lake. Stan hesitated but I was all for it. I was not going to miss anything I wanted to do just because my pregnancy made it more difficult to move around! Besides, I reasoned, if any dangerous conditions occurred that could affect my pregnancy, I could not be in better hands. The pregnancy went well, in spite of my many adventures, and I gave birth to Stanley Jr., the first of our five children, before our year in Philadelphia was over.

We moved to Toledo, Ohio, where Stanley began a four-year residency in obstetrics and gynecology at Toledo Medical Center. We quickly settled into life in this blue-collar city, home to a myriad of diverse cultures.

There was one problem. Medical residents in those days worked long, exhausting hours for just $50 a month! Fortunately, Stanley had savings from his time in general practice, which helped tide us over. To help make ends meet, I arranged to transfer my teaching credentials from Hawaii and took a position at Glenwood Elementary, a K–8 public school where I taught English, social studies, art and biology to students in the seventh and eighth grades. Stan's mother volunteered to join us in Toledo to babysit Stanley Jr. until he was ready for preschool.

We were in fact quite wealthy compared to the medical residents who didn't have other financial resources or childcare support so their wives could seek employment. Every month, on my payday, I invited the residents and their wives to dinner. We all looked forward to our monthly "payday for Pat." It meant a lot to these residents to know they would enjoy a social and free dinner at least one day a month.

Teaching in Toledo was a pleasure in more ways than I expected. As I met my students' families, most of whom were in the butchering business, it felt as though I was the one doing the learning! It was fascinating to discover how these blue-collar, middle-class families with immigrant backgrounds observed their family events and religious commitments.

I was invited to bar mitzvahs, Polish and Irish weddings and other family gatherings. I tasted a variety of ethnic dishes, and especially enjoyed the novelty of Jewish deli food. Having lived most of my life in Hawaii, I found each experience new and exciting. Each added to my appreciation of culturally diverse communities.

In an effort to share some of my own island culture with these generous people, I decided to arrange for a May Day program and offered to teach the children the hula. I was not the most accomplished of dancers, but with proper music from the islands and memories of lessons when I was young, I managed. My parents helped by sending flowers and greenery to create the appropriate ambiance.

Preparations for this program proved to be a big hit with the students, and the dance lessons for both boys and girls had unexpected benefits. There was never a discipline problem in any of my classes, because the students knew poor behavior excluded them from participating. The whole effort was a great success![26]

In late 1958, Stan completed his residency and it was time to go home.

We had three children by then: Stanley Jr., born in Philadelphia, and Sandra and Margaret, born in Toledo. I was pregnant with our fourth child as we drove across the country to ship our car from California to Honolulu.

Stuart was born in March of 1959, "in the Territory of Hawaii," as his birth certificate reads. Five months later, on August 21, President Dwight D. Eisenhower signed a proclamation making Hawaii the 50th state in the union, ending more than half a century of the island's status as a U.S. territory. More than 93 percent of Hawaii voters had approved the statehood proposal. When it became official, people celebrated in the streets—waving flags, playing ukuleles, dancing and proudly displaying the day's Honolulu newspaper headline proclaiming "STATEHOOD!" in giant letters.[27]

As my husband started his new practice in obstetrics and gynecology, one of our first priorities was to find a home. We looked at various houses large enough to meet the needs of our growing family and found exactly what we wanted in the neighborhood of Aina Haina, east of downtown Honolulu. When we made an offer, we were told by the all-white members of the community association that we were not welcome because we were Japanese American. Besides being insulted and hurt, I was shocked to realize this kind of discrimination still existed. We found a suitable home in a different neighborhood, but the sting of that experience fueled my determination to work toward equal opportunity for all. I didn't yet know how, but knew I would find a way.

After some time at home with Stuart, I returned to teaching, this time at Kaimuki Intermediate School,[28] where I was assigned to teach health education to ninth graders. I was there for eight years, during which our youngest child, Laura, was born.

I believe students are most apt to learn and remember facts when they are given dramatic, real-life examples, and I did my best to provide opportunities for that kind of hands-on learning. My students never knew what was in store for them; consequently, there was little absenteeism in my classes.

One day I procured a real cow heart from my butcher. My students were fascinated as we dissected it in class. With an actual specimen to show them, it was easy to explain the various chambers of the heart and its connecting blood vessels. The students found it much more stimulating than looking at a plastic model heart. Of course I had asked my physician husband for some tips before teaching this class. Wearing latex gloves helped quiet the queasiness I felt during this lesson.

The real challenge I faced was teaching the sensitive but necessary topic of sex education. In the 1960s, most parents pretty much relied on the schools to tackle that subject. I suspect that remains true today.

The Department of Education didn't provide a lesson plan, so we were left to be cautiously creative in explaining procreation. My approach was to answer questions in a matter-of-fact manner, always using the proper scientific terminology for body parts and functions. I guess I made an impression on these ninth graders; decades later, I bumped into a former student who remembered me because of my lesson explaining the purpose of semen. He said he was grateful for my careful explanation. I didn't ask why!

The Call to Action

Teachers were subject to rules and regulations set by the Department of Education and the prerogatives of school principals, who set policies and procedures. In those days, we had no choice but to comply; there were no unions or organizations for teachers to go to for relief when priorities conflicted. I became increasingly distressed by a number of practices that affected not just me, but all of my fellow teachers.

The Department of Education forced teachers to identify students by category. They called it "tracking." Students were evaluated at the eighth-grade level and placed in one of two tracks: One group, considered outstanding/superior/college material, was guided into college-preparatory courses. The second group, considered medium/slower students, were seen as trade school material and given home economics or shop as more suitable courses.

I felt neither prepared nor qualified to determine the future of students by tracking them at such an early age. As a teacher, I knew there were normal variations in the pacing of each child's development and skills mastery. I could not in good conscience deny "slower" students an opportunity for higher education.

I certainly would not want my own children, at the tender age of 13 or 14, to be subjected to one teacher's determination of their future! I deeply resented the tracking requirement and as an eighth grade homeroom teacher did not comply.

Teachers were subjected to other demands not always associated with education. We had no free time for lesson planning. We were required to monitor recess, which meant we never had a break. There was no special place to rest or make phone calls. There was no freedom to try new teaching methods, like team teaching.

The blow that finally drove me to action occurred when Laura, who was attending a nearby preschool, fell ill. I was in my classroom when I got a notice from the office at my school that she had been taken to the hospital. Of course I immediately rushed to the office, hoping to use the phone to check on her condition. I was told it was against regulations for teachers to use school phones for personal business, but I was welcome to use the public phone up the street on 18th Avenue. I was mortified!

Once the crisis had passed, I made another phone call—to Charles "Charlie" Kendall, then executive director and CEO of the Hawaii

Government Employees Association (HGEA).[29] I approached him on the basis that public school teachers are government workers and should have representation by an organization. Neither the Hawaii State Teachers Association nor the Hawaii Federation of Teachers were in existence in Hawaii at that time.[30]

From that phone call, the Teachers' Chapter of the HGEA was born. Charlie came to my home the next day. We sat on my lanai and drafted a contract creating the new chapter, which some call the first teachers' union in Hawaii. We were told the Teachers' Chapter would have the full support of the HGEA and its board of directors. In fact, we were assured a seat on the board. So we were confident the board would "have our backs" whenever we testified at the state legislature on behalf of teachers.

With the help of many other concerned teachers, I recruited more than 2,000 eager educators to form the first Teachers' Chapter of the HGEA. You'd be amazed how quickly the news spread from teacher to teacher in those days before cell phones and social media. It was an easy sell. Teachers were head-over-heels ecstatic at the prospect of having representation after all the years of being denied basic rights to which other government employees were entitled.

With the enthusiastic support of my fellow teachers, I became chairman of this new chapter. I took a seat on the Board of the Directors of the HGEA and became the teachers' spokesperson at the state legislature.

We worked together to seek needed changes to allow teachers to be considered professionals and given the respect and privileges they deserved. Teachers' rooms eventually were created in every school, with access to telephones for private calls. A free period for planning was built into the school day and relief from playground duties would come later.

This was my first experience with effecting change through the political system. I will always be grateful for the foresight and support of Charlie Kendall, who rightfully has a building—an office condominium close to state and county offices in downtown Honolulu[31]—named after him. His immediate successors as head of the HGEA, David K. Trask Jr.[32] and Daniel Ainoa,[33] also were supportive of the Teachers' Chapter.

Learning Through Involvement

In 1967 I took a position at Kalani High School, where I taught "American Problems," a fancy title for social studies. The curriculum included a unit on government, and I thought the best way for students to learn how laws are made would be to involve them in the process. In 1969, the Hawaii state legislature was discussing the possibility of lowering the voting age for state elections from 21 to 18.[34] I knew the issue would resonate with my students, who of course believed strongly that they should be able to vote when they became 18. So I challenged them: Tell me why you feel this way and I'll arrange for you to go testify at the legislative committee hearing. They were delighted!

Thanks to friends on the committee, I was able to arrange an opportunity for my students to testify and participate in the process of enacting legislation.

Imagine their elation when the measure was approved by the full state legislature! As a proposed amendment to the state constitution, however, Senate Bill 170 required voter approval. It failed to gain sufficient support from the electorate when offered to voters in November 1970.[35] However, the measure ultimately passed. Congress also approved the Twenty-Sixth Amendment, which lowered the federal voting age to 18, in 1971. It was quickly ratified by the states, and President Richard Nixon signed the measure into law in July 1971.

My students left this experience with a much greater understanding of, and interest in, the state legislative process. Everything they read in their books about state government made more sense to them, and teaching government was easier and more fulfilling for me because I knew I had captured their interest.

From 1966 to 1968, I also volunteered in the Republican minority office at the state legislature. It was a pleasure to work with leaders such as Dominis Garida ("D. G." or "Andy") Anderson,[36] Fred Rohlf-ing,[37] Wadsworth Y. H. Yee[38] and Ambrose Rosehill.[39] As a research assistant, I worked on testimony and developed strategy on various issues—often with a focus on education.

It was interesting work but I grew increasingly frustrated when many of my own ideas were simply put on hold. This was when it started to dawn on me that I could run for office myself, and work to see some of my ideas implemented through legislation.

After a while, Republican leaders decided my involvement as a Republican Party official would be helpful. On a Saturday morning in May of 1967, I got a telephone call from Fred Rohlfing, who asked me to take an early flight to Maui, where the party's state convention was being held. I was recruited to run for secretary of the Hawaii Republican Party and rounded up the votes needed to elect me to the position.

About two years after I first started volunteering for the Republican Party, I decided to run for a position as a delegate to the first state constitutional convention in 1968. The ConCon was held nine years after statehood. I knew this convention would determine the future of our state. I diligently did my homework, offered myself as a candidate and learned to campaign door to door, meeting people, drafting brochures and doing all things political to get elected.

I was thrilled to win election to this august body, and the experience was unforgettable. We passed the State of Hawaii's very first constitution since statehood, formalizing all branches of government, establishing Neighbor Island political entities and setting reapportionment standards for future elections. It was a genuinely nonpartisan effort and involved leaders from both political parties who laid aside partisan interests for the good of the state. In fact, Hebden Porteus, a Republican who was then president of the state Senate, was elected president of the Convention. All who participated were true statesmen, and the most important document in our young state's history was written. 🖋

Pat Saiki's mother, Shizue Fukuda, designed and sewed her daughter's gown for the 1949 Kapalapala Beauty Pageant sight unseen, without taking a single measurement. It fit perfectly.

Top: *The 1949 Kapalapala Beauty Pageant contestants, from left: Sally Debelles, Edmee Jones, Gloria Kanemura, Patricia Fukuda (Saiki), Annie Lee and Miriam Tseu.* **Bottom left:** *Pat's first election victory: delegate to the state's first constitutional convention in 1968.* **Bottom right:** *The Saiki family, left to right standing: Pat, Stanley Jr., Dr. Stanley Saiki, Laura, Stuart, Margaret, and at the keyboard, Sandra.*

Left: Grandparents Yusu and Matsuzo Fukuda. ***Right:*** Pat (in uniform) worked
her way through the University of Hawaii as a part-time flight attendant for
Aloha Airlines. In this photo she is with her younger sister, June.

PART I ENDNOTES

1   Pat's middle name, Hatsue, means "firstborn daughter."

2   "In 1884, Hawai'i Island was home to 24,991 residents and more than 30 sugar plantations, many of which were in East Hawai'i. With demand far outweighing the available workforce, thousands of workers were imported, usually from Asia, to work the cane fields." Denise Laitinen, "Then and Now: Hilo Sugar Mill/Wainaku Center," *Ke Ola Magazine*, September/October 2013, https://keolamagazine.com/then-now/hilo-sugar-mill-wainaku-center/.

3   "According to an 1897 report from the Secretary of the Bureau of Immigration, Hawai'i Island had 9,680 sugar plantation laborers—more than any other island in the state. The workers were a diverse lot: 425 were Hawaiian; 952 were Portuguese; 5,021 were Japanese; 2,995 were Chinese; with 20 South Sea Islanders, and 267 others … "Situated on the sea cliffs just north of Hilo and tucked behind old concrete walls is the former Hilo Sugar Mill, which in its heyday processed 1,400 tons of sugar a day." Denise Laitinen, "Then and Now: Hilo Sugar Mill/Wainaku Center," *Ke Ola Magazine*, September/October 2013, https://keolamagazine.com/then-now/hilo-sugar-mill-wainaku-center/.

4   Patsy Sumie Saiki (no relation), *Japanese Women in Hawaii: The First 100 Years* (Honolulu: Kisaku, 1985), 127.

5   This family-owned store shut its doors in 1996, after 85 years in downtown Hilo. Kimberly A. Carter, "Hilo old-timers bid farewell to landmark Ah Mai store," *Star-Bulletin*, http://archives.starbulletin.com/96/10/07/news/story2.html.

6   By 1938, Hilo Sugar Mill had built 52 miles of permanent water flumes and 15 miles of portable flumes. Denise Laitinen, "Then and Now: Hilo Sugar Mill/Wainaku Center," *Ke Ola Magazine*, September/October 2013, https://keolamagazine.com/then-now/hilo-sugar-mill-wainaku-center/.

7   Hawaii was at that time still a U.S. territory. It did not become a state until 1959.

8   Ray, M., "Executive Order 9066," *Encyclopedia Britannica*, last modified June 19, 2018. https://www.britannica.com/topic/Executive-Order-9066.

9   "Because Japanese Americans were crucial to the economic health of Hawaii, the FBI detained only the leaders of the Japanese, German, and Italian-American communities after the bombing of Pearl Harbor. No one was ever found guilty of a crime. … "The Japanese Cultural Center of Hawaii (JCCH) produced the documentary, 'The Untold Story: Internment of Japanese Americans in Hawai'i,' as part of the effort to preserve the national memory." "The Untold Story: Japanese-Americans' WWII Interment in Hawaii," NBCNews.com, https://www.nbcnews.com/news/asian-america/untold-storyjapa-nese-americans-wwii-in-ternment-hawaii-n170746.

10 The Honouliuli Internment Camp on Oahu, now a National Historic Site, was Hawaii's largest and longest-operating internment camp. It opened in 1943 and closed in 1946. "History & Culture – Honouliuli National Historic Site," National Park Service, last modified January 4, 2017, https://www.nps.gov/hono/learn/historyculture/index.htm.

11 "History & Culture – Honouliuli National Historic Site," National Park Service, last modified January 4, 2017, https://www.nps.gov/hono/learn/historyculture/index.htm.

12 Don Wallace, "7 Things about Hawaii's Largest Internment Camp That May Surprise You," *Honolulu* magazine, March 31, 2015, http://www.honolulumagazine.com/Honolulu-

Magazine/March-2015/7-Things-About-Hawaiis-Largest-Internment-Camp-That-May-Surprise-You/.

13 Honouliuli Internment Camp: https://historichawaii.org/2014/02/19/honouliuli-internment-camp/.

14 "Tsunamis—large sea waves generated by earthquakes, underwater landslides and other disturbances—aren't common occurrences in Hawaii. However, when they do happen, Hilo Bay on the Big Island has often been subject to the worst of their devastating effects. The funnel-like underwater shape of Hilo's bayfront amplifies the incoming waves creating larger heights, stronger inland surges." Vanessa Sim, "Three tsunamis that changed Hilo and the Big Island," *Hawai'i Magazine*, November 25, 2009, https://www.hawaiimagazine.com/blogs/hawaii_today/2009/11/25/tsunami_Hilo_Big_Island_Hawaii.

15 Mary Vorsino, "70 years on, April Fools' Day tsunami painful reminder of ocean's destructive force," Hawaii News Now, April 1, 2016 (updated September 20), https://www.hawaiinewsnow.com/story/31624669/70-years-on-april-fools-day-tsunami-painful-reminder-of-oceans-destructive-force/.

16 Shinmachi tsunami: https://ui.adsabs.harvard.edu/abs/2016AGUFMNH43A1800C/abstract.

17 "Uncover the history of Shinmachi at the Lyman," *Hawaii Tribune-Herald*, October 12, 2019, https://www.hawaiitribune-herald.com/2019/10/12/community/uncover-the-history-of-shinmachi-at-the-lyman/.

18 Michael Brestovansky, "Researcher documents the story of Shinmachi," *Hawaii Tribune-Herald*, May 20,2019, https://www.hawaiitribuneherald.com/2019/05/20/hawaii-news/researcher-documents-the-story-of-shinmachi/.

19 Vanessa Sim, "Three tsunamis that changed Hilo and Hawaii's Big Island," *Hawai'i Magazine*, November 25, 2009, https://www.hawaiimagazine.com/blogs/hawaii_today/2009/11/25/tsunami_Hilo_Big_Island_Hawaii.

20 Tsunami Warning System: https://earthweb.ess.washington.edu/tsunami/general/historic/aleutian46.html.

21 Ruddy Tongg: https://tim.hawaii.edu/about-values-vision-mission-accreditation/celebrate-a-legacy-in-tourism/2009-celebrate-a-legacy-in-tourism-honorees/ruddy-tongg/.

22 The makai side [of Sacred Hearts Covenant School] became the Ritz Department Store in 1954. http://fortstreetmall.org/historic-buildings/

23 History of Punahou: https://www.punahou.edu/about/history-and-traditions.

24 Nearly two decades years later, a young man who went by the name of Barry Soetoro attended Punahou. As Barack Obama (his original name), he served as the 44th president of the United States from January 20, 2009, to January 20, 2017.

25 One of Higgins's student athletes was Betty Ann Barnett (class of 1964), who was inducted into the Hawaii Swimming Hall of Fame in 2008 in two categories: Masters and Ocean Swimmers. "At Punahou, Barnett started swimming in the third grade under the watchful and encouraging eyes of Rolland 'Rollie' Higgins. She joined the swim team, and pool competition quickly followed. 'Higgins recognized a natural ability in me and guided me during my developing years,' said Barnett, who also credits the coach for helping her perfect her swim strokes and encouraging her to excel." www.punahou.edu

26 In a letter to "Mrs. Saiki's Class," dated May 7, 1958, Leona Probst, junior high supervisor for the Toledo Board of Education, complimented the children on their performance, acknowledging, "You certainly had to learn a great deal about Hawaii (music, dances, customs, clothes, language, etc.) in order to put on such an interesting, authentic program." After offering very specific praise for the graceful dances, expressive hand interpretations and parts played "with dignity and poise," she wrote, "I'm sure, as you think back over your junior high school years, this experience will always stand out in your memory as one of the finest."

27 Statehood: https://www.youtube.com/watch?v=xNnNHpkbjbo and https://www.bigis-landtv.com/history/hawaiian-statehood-1959/.

28 Now called Kaimuki Middle School.

29 Kendall was first elected HGEA president in 1937 and was named ED/CEO in 1946. https://www.hgea.org/our-union/history-milestones/

30 HSTA wasn't incorporated until 1971. https://www.hsta.org/about-us/history.

31 Kendall Building: http://choi.hawaiilife.com/prop/downtown/888-mililani-street-ph-4-ho-nolulu-hi-96813-201819068.

32 David K. Trask Jr. led the effort to transition HGEA from an employee association to a union with the constitutional convention passage of bargaining for public employees and the passage of Chapter 89 HRS (https://www.hgea.org/news/2016/february/19/hgea-saddened-by-the-death-of-david-k-trask-jr/). In 1954, five years before statehood, Trask was part of a wave of Democrat candidates who swept into the Hawaii House of Representatives. The Senate was taken over by Democrats two years later.

33 Trask's successor, and apparently someone with whom Trask did not always agree. "Trask felt that becoming part of a larger union was a positive thing; HGEA deputy director Dan Ainoa did not. It was the start of a long-running tug-of-war between Ainoa and Trask that ended when Trask was fired in 1967." When Ainoa retired, Trask replaced him.

34 The long debate over lowering the voting age in America from 21 to 18 began during World War II and intensified during the Vietnam War, when young men denied the right to vote were being conscripted to fight for their country. In the 1970 case *Oregon v. Mitchell*, a divided U.S. Supreme Court ruled that Congress had the right to regulate the minimum age in federal elections, but not at the state and local level. Amid increasing support for a constitutional amendment, Congress passed the Twenty-sixth Amendment in March 1971; the states promptly ratified it, and President Richard M. Nixon signed it into law that July. https://www.history.com/topics/united-states-constitution/the-26th-amendment

35 Acts from the 1969 SLH (the proposed constitutional amendment is on page 521 of the pdf): https://www.capitol.hawaii.gov/slh/AllIndex/All_Acts_SLH1969.pdf. The voting age was changed to 18 years in 1973. Act 217, SLH 1973: https://www.capitol.hawaii.gov/slh/Years/SLH1973/SLH1973_Act217.pdf.

36 Dominis Garrida Anderson was a self-made success in real estate development and restaurants. He served in both the House and Senate. Kevin Dayton, "Andy Anderson: Tough, practical and 'sassy'," *Honolulu Advertiser*, September 5, 2002, http://the.honolu-luadvertiser.com/article/2002/Sep/05/ln/ln09a.html.

37 Fred Rohlfing, an attorney, served 21 years in the state House and Senate. A Republican in a blue state who was "loved by many." Retired to Maui, where he served as counsel to the Maui County corporation council. He died at the age of 89 from complications of

Parkinson's disease. Melissa Tanji, "Former Maui County corporation counsel Fred Rohlf-ing dies at 89," The Maui News, August 16, 2018, https://www.mauinews.com/news/local-news/2018/08/former-maui-county-corporation-counsel-fred-rohlfing-dies-at-89/.

38 Wadsworth Y. H. Yee was an attorney and land developer who served in territorial House and state House from 1958 to 1962. He served in the state Senate from 1966 to 1982, until he was defeated by Democrat Neil Abercrombie. https://www.newspapers.com/clip/17411768/wadsworth-yee-obit/

39 Ambrose Rosehill: "The young Honolulu attorney was an up-and-coming GOP star and hoped to breathe new life into the Republican Party with his more independent-leaning ideas. He ran his first campaign for the Territorial Legislature in 1958, along with a group of other young and ambitious Republicans, none of whom had much financial back-ing. He won and was re-elected three times." Loren Moreno, "Former judge Ambrose Rosehill," September 20, 2006, http://the.honoluluadvertiser.com/article/2006/Sep/20/ln/FP609200346.html.

Pat and her father, Kazuo Fukuda, going door-to-door during the campaign for a seat in the state House of Representatives.

PART II

The State House and Senate Years 1968–1983

Running for Office

Shortly after the Constitutional Convention, my fellow teachers and constituents asked me to run for Hawaii's House of Representatives. I was very hesitant because my five children were still very young, ranging in age from six to 14. I felt conflicted. Shouldn't my role at this time be homemaker?

It was my husband and my eldest son, Stan Jr., and my parents, Kazuo and Shizue Fukuda in Hilo, who convinced me that I should go for it—and of course, they offered to share the burden of family obligations. It was not an easy decision, but relying on their offers of help, I filed a nomination application indicating my intention to run in the 1968 election to become a state representative from the 17th House district, an area encompassing Palolo, St. Louis Heights, part of Kapahulu, Kaimuki, Waialae-Kahala and Kahala.

My decision to run also had roots in personal history. The overt discrimination my husband and I faced when we were denied home ownership, the changes I knew were needed in the educational system and my own experience with schoolteacher mistreatment incentivized me to overturn the "status quo."

Many friends and acquaintances questioned why I chose to run as a Republican when the overwhelming majority of Hawaii voters were Democrats.[1] My Democrat friends did try to persuade me to join their party. I would have been welcomed by those in power and seeking Democrat votes certainly would have been much easier for me.

My decision came down to basics. I believed in the Republican principles of limited government, individual freedom and fiscal responsibility. The platform of a more conservative approach to spending taxpayer funds also intrigued me. Perhaps because of my childhood experience in Hilo, where the *kumiai* tradition pulled communities together in the name of mutual support and sustainability, I was disturbed to see the strong entitlement tendency in people who depended solely on the government to solve all problems and fund all projects.

Most importantly, I believed then, and still do, that a strong two-party system is in the long run most beneficial for the people of our state. In the years since statehood, Democrats had dominated the governorship, the state legislature and three of Hawaii's four congressional seats.[2] Overwhelmingly disproportionate influence and longstanding rule by one political party can lead to favoritism and corruption. The one-party system in Hawaii needed to be challenged—otherwise collusion, manipulation and outright abuse of power were inevitable.

Competition, I felt, was better. It assured people that all voices and political positions would be heard and better decisions would result. The challenge posed by robust opposition demands accountability of incumbent politicians. An effective Republican Party would provide vigilant watchdogs and alternative solutions to problems. For all of those reasons, I chose the harder path to election.

The decision to run as a Republican wasn't my only challenge to attaining office. At that time, of the 51 members in the state House of Representatives, only three were women.[3] Dorothy Devereux, the only Republican woman in the House, represented District 15. Democrat women in the House included Momi T. Minn,[4] who represented the Waianae area of Honolulu County (District 10) and Sarah K. M. Pule, a former teacher's aide and Hawaiian language translator who had been appointed to represent District 5 by Governor John A. Burns after her husband, former Big Island representative Akoni Pule, retired in ill health in 1969.[5] Republican Eureka Forbes was the only woman in the 25-member state Senate.[6]

My district had always been represented by men.[7] I seized upon that, insisting "We Need a Woman in the House" in my campaign theme.

Elections cost money. You need a "walk piece" that introduces who you are and why you are running. You need to pay for printing and postage to send mass mailers to reach every household in your district. You need yard signs and signs that supporters can wave by hand. Refreshments for volunteers are always welcome.

I was fortunate to have top-notch campaign and finance teams. Raymond M. Torkildson,[8] a well-known and respected attorney who also was a good friend, took on the responsibility of campaign chair. His campaign finance team included Roy King, then a vice president of First Hawaiian Bank, and James Napier,[9] a rancher and member of the Hawaii Cattlemen's Council. I also had many loyal friends, both personally and professionally, who stepped forward to support me.

Roy, who was a good friend and neighbor, offered the use of his vintage Ford convertible, bedecked with balloons. As we drove across the district, waving and chatting with constituents, we made many friends.

Thanks to invaluable help of friends like these and a legion of volunteers, I won my first legislative race. On election night, once it became clear I was going to win, the excitement of the moment gave way to humility that so many people had voted for me, and awe in seeing the democratic process at work. I never lost that feeling of pride in our American way of governance, regardless of whether I won or lost, in every election I contested over the next three decades.

Focusing on Work and Family

Now there were four women in the state House of Representatives. I requested and was assigned to the committees on education, higher education and health. There was much to be done in all of these areas, and so much to tackle.

All these years later, what I remember most vividly from that first term in office is how much effort was required on the home front so I could be an effective legislator. Many people asked how I managed to attend to my family while serving as a legislator, especially when we were in session. It wasn't easy—it took discipline, planning and quite a bit of juggling—but I always kept in mind that my first priority was my family.

I spent every weekend freezing dinners so that the family would always have nutritious meals. When the legislature was in session, I let leaders know that I would be absent from 4 to 6 p.m. every day so I could pick up my youngest from elementary school. They knew not to schedule late-afternoon votes if they needed my support. I made parent-teacher conferences a priority and always emphasized to my children's teachers that they should not hesitate to reach out to me with questions or concerns. I didn't want them to think that my job as a state legislator took priority over being an engaged and attentive mom.

At home, my oldest daughter, Sandra, was a big help. She defrosted the dinners I had prepared and got things ready for the evening meal.

It was during this first term that I got to know Miriam Hellreich, who would go on to become a long-serving Republican national committeewoman from Hawaii and a board member of public institutions including the East-West Center in Hawaii and the national Corporation for Public Broadcasting. In those days, however, Miriam was an activist and, like me, a young mother. During one of her visits to my office, I asked Miriam, "Do you know anything about microwave ovens?" These were the latest in kitchen appliances and offered my poor family the possibility of salvation from burnt, reheated meals prepared by my well-intentioned kids.

Everyone cooperated at home, including my physician husband. It took a team effort to make things work. No doubt every member of my family made sacrifices along the way, but they always supported what I was doing because they knew the effort was worthwhile.

Any challenges I faced in this juggling act were certainly not mine alone. Working women all across the nation, in all types of careers, were struggling in their efforts to "do it all." Resentment simmered as more and more women realized their contributions were not valued, nor their work compensated, at levels equal to men.

A national movement was underway to recognize equal rights for women in America. The movement attracted attention by way of those infamous "bra-burning" episodes and large-scale demonstrations demanding gender equality under the law.

In August 1969, toward the end of my first term as a legislator, President Richard M. Nixon, having learned of my interest and leadership on this subject in Hawaii, appointed me to his Advisory Council on the Status of Women.[10] This group met in Washington, D.C., on several occasions and spearheaded a renewed effort to add the Equal Rights Amendment to the U.S. Constitution.[11]

The Abortion Controversy

In 1970, one of the biggest controversies nationwide was whether a woman should have the right to terminate an unwanted pregnancy.

It would be three years before the U.S. Supreme Court made its historic decision, in *Roe v. Wade*, to affirm a woman's right to an abortion under the Fourteenth Amendment to the Constitution. But in March 1970, Hawaii and New York became the first two states in the U.S. to decriminalize it.

The issue was introduced in the Hawaii Senate on February 10, 1970, by Senator Vincent Yano,[12] chairman of the Public Health Committee, who, despite being a devout Roman Catholic, believed women should have the right to decide what happens to their own bodies.

Making *all* abortions legal was never the intent of the legislation, called Hawaii's Freedom of Choice Act. The measure would allow any woman who had lived in Hawaii for at least 90 days to have a legal abortion—performed by a licensed physician or osteopath, in a hospital licensed by the state or federal government—if the embryo or fetus was "nonviable," interpreted by legislative lawyers at that time to mean the first four or five months of pregnancy. The proposal would allow civil action if a viable fetus were killed through negligent or criminal acts.

Much discussion ensued, with Governor John Burns—another devout Catholic—remaining silent. Activists on both sides of the issue were similar to those all over the mainland. Our state became very divided, with religious entities vehemently opposed to abortion rights and women's groups just as vehemently in favor of them.

I entered the controversy with an opinion influenced by the selfless courage of my obstetrician/gynecologist husband. Stanley was deeply devoted to his patients and he always took extraordinary care in attending to their every need.

On more than one occasion, he would receive a call—usually between 2 and 4 a.m.—from a patient who was bleeding profusely because of an illegal abortion performed by a "coat hanger" artist under horrible, unclean and infectious circumstances.

What was this dedicated doctor to do? If he did anything to stop the bleeding, if he gave any assistance at all, he could be arrested for aiding and abetting an abortion, which was illegal under the existing state law.

The woman had already made her decision. And no matter why she chose an abortion, my husband believed that saving her life was more important than the risk he took in breaking the law. I supported him in that conviction, and I joined him when he met these patients at his medical office. I had the sobering task of holding a lamp over the woman so Stanley could see what he was doing. Switching on the office lights was out of the question because it would signal to police that something out of the ordinary was happening. We all—my husband, the patient and I—could be arrested for breaking the law.

Each high-risk operation meant a woman's life was saved. That outcome was enough for my husband, but it was not enough for me. I was outraged to know that a trained physician and his patient could be so unfairly exposed to prosecution. Beyond that, the woman deserved better—she shouldn't be punished for making a difficult choice and she certainly shouldn't be exposed to unsanitary medical practices by an illegal abortionist.

I took this message to my colleagues in the state House and asked them to consider that a woman's choice should be her own. As the mother of five children, I could only imagine how heart-wrenching a decision to abort a pregnancy would be. But I strongly believed that first-trimester abortions chosen for medical reasons—to save the life of a mother, or to terminate a pregnancy that results from rape or incest—should be legally accessible and performed by a licensed physician in a hospital setting.

I never supported the full-scale legalization of abortion, but I have always supported the right of a woman to choose what happens to her body. Let's give some credit to women that they are capable of making such difficult decisions thoughtfully, and with full consideration of their life circumstances.

By February 24, 1970, Hawaii's Freedom of Choice Act had cleared both the House and the Senate.[13] The bill, described in *The New York Times* as "the most liberal of any in the nation," was enacted without the signature of the governor, who for personal and religious reasons chose not to sign it.[14]

I feel a great sense of satisfaction knowing I participated in this effort— despite occasional harassment by opponents who accused me of being an "abortionist." Many others have been chastised for supporting this humane effort to save women's lives. Hawaii legislation meets the needs of our community and I am proud of having played a part in its passage. My colleagues, especially Senator Vincent Yano, the bill's author, should be hailed for their insight.

In retrospect, I would have strongly favored the passage of specific legislation criminalizing unlicensed abortion practitioners and holding harmless physicians who saved the victims of botched abortions.

Back on the Campaign Trail

In the fall of 1970, I ran for reelection to the state House. In addition to retaining my winning campaign team from before, I recruited Dr. Franklin Kometani,[15] a well-known dentist whose father, also a dentist, was prominent in the Japanese American community and a familiar name in the corridors of power. Frank had gained valuable experience that year working on Senator Hebden Porteus's Republican primary campaign for governor. He brought that experience to my campaign in the general election, serving as chairman. It was a role that Frank reprised many times in the coming years.

Besides walking door-to-door, leaving brochures when people were not at home and waving signs on the highway, we set up a telephone bank in my garage, where volunteers made phone calls to engage people at home. This had to be done in the early evening, so it meant running home and fixing snacks to get everyone through the evening.

As we got closer to November 4, we turned our focus to reminding people to vote. We reached out to individuals with absentee ballots and reminded them to mail them in. On Election Day we made calls to make sure people could get to the polls. If anyone needed a ride, we sent volunteers to chauffeur them.

Once again, a majority of voters in the 17th House District trusted me to represent their interests in the Hawaii state legislature. In January 1971, I began my second term in the Hawaii House of Representatives.

Equal Rights for Women

A year later, as the nationwide focus on women's rights continued to pick up steam, I launched a local push for equal rights legislation for women. In what the *Honolulu Advertiser* described as a "nice touch of irony," I announced my intention the same day my fellow female legislator, Senator Eureka Forbes,[16] was barred from eating lunch with her male colleagues in a dining hall often referred to as "the stag room."[17]

It was one example of many common slights—some subtle, some

obvious, all odious—that women in the 1970s faced on a daily basis.

Back then, a woman could not have a credit card in her own name. I remember calling Diner's Club, a national credit card organization, to request my own card. My call was handled with courtesy, but I was informed that company policy required my husband's name on the card. Even after I explained that I was the traveler who used the card, they were adamant that my husband's name was needed. They tried to sell me a "spouse" card, but that required my husband to shoulder all legal and financial responsibility for my charges. I had my own salary, and I was just as financially responsible as he was! I persisted, and finally got the card, but I believe being a state representative had something to do with my success.

In those days, women could not own mortgages in their own names. (Archaic barriers of supposed risk included simply being of "impregnable" age.)

Pregnant women were forced to take maternity leave without pay and with no guarantee of re-employment. They could collect unemployment insurance payments only for the four months leading up to their child's birth and the two months afterward. If they returned to work, they had to prove their children and households would be adequately cared for.

I was outraged that women were forced to provide more evidence to an employer to return to work than a man would have to do. I also felt strongly that the privacy of a family's financial decisions and priorities should be respected.

Pat Putman of the Legislative Reference Bureau volunteered to conduct exhaustive research to unearth any and all Hawaii laws that discriminated against women. Over the next few months we developed a package of 28 bills to address these inequities and introduced them in the legislature as my Equal Rights Package. The bills gained a "women's rights" label, but I preferred to phrase them as "people's rights."[18] Among the proposals:[19]

- Civil service workers would get paid maternity leave for six weeks before and after birth and could apply unused sick leave pay toward time they otherwise would have to take as unpaid maternity leave.

- Women who were unable to work because of an illness associated with pregnancy would be entitled to temporary disability insurance.
- Homemakers returning to work would no longer be required to prove that their households would be taken care of while they were on the job. Wage rates for female employees could no longer be determined by the lowest rate paid to male workers.
- Men and women would have equal inheritance rights for state pensions. A woman's legal will would remain valid after her marriage.
- A woman could, but was not required to, take her husband's last name after marriage.

One bill called for repeal of a little-known law to prevent "unmarried girls under 16" to "loiter" on the streets of Hilo or Honolulu between the hours of 8 p.m. and 4 a.m. A number of bills moved to strike the words "woman," "female," "widow" and "father" from legislation, instead inserting "spouse," "person" or "parent."

And then there was this appalling situation: A wife who was abused by her husband could not bring charges against him. She could complain to the police but had no recourse through the courts. We amended the law to include spouse abuse as a misdemeanor, allowing victims to initiate action in family court.

These are only a few examples of the egregious laws on the books and the many injustices I worked to correct in an effort to provide equality and protection under the law.

The U.S. House had passed the Equal Rights Amendment on October 12, 1971.[20] On March 22, 1972, when it was approved by the U.S. Senate, it was sent to the states for ratification. To be added to the U.S. Constitution, the amendment needed approval by legislatures in three-fourths (38) of the 50 states.[21]

In Hawaii, I introduced legislation in the House that would add the Equal Rights Amendment to our state constitution and asked Democrat senator John Ushijima of the Big Island to introduce a companion bill in the Senate.

Seeking his support was a practical, and necessary, move. Local practices, still prevalent in our state legislature, prevent any bill introduced by the minority party to become law. I knew Senator Ushijima and his wife were avid supporters of this Equal Rights Amendment. With their help and that of many outspoken, high-profile women, the measure passed overwhelmingly. We became the first state in the nation to ratify the Equal Rights Amendment.

That was just the beginning. From 1972 to 1975, with similar efforts of collaboration to overcome barriers I faced as a member of the minority party, 25 of my equal-rights bills passed both chambers of the state legislature and became law. Because of the partisanship, of course, Democrats got all the credit. Thankfully, several diligent newspaper reporters looked beyond the official press releases and wrote stories acknowledging my involvement.

One example appeared in an article by political reporter Gerry Keir, whose March 14, 1973 story in the *Honolulu Advertiser* had a headline that said, "GOP bill goes through under Demo banner." As the story explained, "The Democrat controlled State House yesterday passed a disguised Republican bill wiping out an 'anti-housewife' clause in Hawaii's unemployment benefits law. But, just to keep their partisan record intact, Democrats 'laundered' the bill beforehand — introducing it, in identical language, under the signatures of Democrat lawmakers."

It further revealed that "...the switch did not escape the notice of the GOP minority, which holds 16 of the 51 House seats. Republicans called attention to the legislative credit grab—labeling it 'political shenanigans.' "

Everyone knew I was the author of that measure, which was part of my Equal Rights Package. When it was resurrected under the name of the Democrat chairman of the House Labor Committee, Oliver Lunasco, Minority Floor Leader Joseph Garcia Jr. led a charge to rectify the credit grab. He gave a convincing and pointed speech calling out the shameful behavior, but to no avail. The committee voted down my bill by voice vote, instead moving Lunasco's measure to a full House vote.

I didn't want a fight about who got credit for it preventing this important measure from being enacted. I wanted the bill to pass. So, I supported Lunasco's bill, which was essentially my own bill. It mattered more to me that the measure passed than that I received credit for initiating it.

We were fortunate that over the years nonpartisan journalists reported matters as they saw them. Gerry Keir, Tom Horton, Jerry Burris, Andy Yamaguchi and Floyd Takeuchi at the *Honolulu Advertiser* and Cobey Black, Gregg Kakesako, Doug Boswell, Hildegaard Verploegen and Richard Borecca of the *Honolulu Star-Bulletin* were some of the reporters who got it right. They gave credit where credit was due. In their stories, at least, I was named author of the bills giving equal rights to women.

Of the many injustices the new legislation addressed, correcting the credit card discrimination proved easiest to accomplish. I placed a call to Henry A. Walker Jr., president and CEO of Amfac, the oldest and at that time the largest corporation in Hawaii.[22] Among its many holdings, Amfac owned and ran Liberty House, one of the most respected and popular department stores in the state. It later was acquired by Federated Department Stores and was rebranded as Macy's.[23]

Walker was shocked to learn that women who shopped at Liberty House had been forced to list their husbands as principal owners of the store's credit card accounts. He moved to correct that immediately, leading the way for other stores and establishments to follow suit. And they did, setting a trend that would soon be followed by local and mainland retailers. After this breakthrough, the dam was breached.

Today, we can hardly keep the credit card companies away. Women can borrow money and own real estate in their own names. For real and sometimes cosmetic reasons, our vocabulary around certain professional roles changed.

Salesmen became salespersons, policemen became police officers, firemen became firefighters, etc.

But deeply ingrained habits don't change overnight. I learned through friends that discrimination was rampant in some of the more "exclusive" sectors of society. Some women approached me seeking assistance with discriminatory rules prohibiting them from becoming members at the prestigious Waialae Country Club.[24] The equal protection clause of our state constitution says there can be "no discrimination according to race, religion or sex" in a public facility. But because Waialae was a private club, it was under no obligation to adhere to that edict.

I found a way around it.

The club was located close to Diamond Head State Monument, on prime residential land in Kahala, home of the wealthy. The club's developers had sought and received zoning dispensation from the Honolulu Department of Planning and Permitting, changing the land use permit from residential to "open space," which allowed them to locate their private golf course on the parcel of prime real estate.

In 1973, I drafted legislation that would change the designation of the land back from "open space" to "residential," hoping to pressure the club to change its discriminatory rule and allow women to become members. I took the bill to Senator Hebden Porteus, who, coincidentally, also served as chairman of the board of directors at Waialae. He recognized the discrimination, and the threat my bill posed to the club. Even if it didn't pass, the publicity from introducing it could be damaging to the club's reputation and membership.

I assured Hebden that was not my intent but insisted the rule against membership for women be changed. He astutely called an emergency meeting of the club's rules committee, which quickly decided to open membership to women.

Nearly a decade later, a similar, but quieter, behind-the-scenes battle ensued, this time with the Pacific Club, which as late as 1982 was still denying full membership to women. (Eileen Anderson, Honolulu's first woman mayor, had been named an "honorary" member of the club—an honor she refused because of the club's stand against women members.[25])

The situation was called to my attention by, of all people, the daughter of my friend and mentor Henry Walker, the Amfac executive who had helped me resolve the credit card problem at Liberty House. He was, coincidentally, very influential with the Pacific Club's board. When his daughter Susan solicited my help, I thought a public display with the two of us laying our bodies at the front door of the club might be sufficient to force change. In fact, simply informing Henry of our plans was enough. The problem was solved without causing a scandal. Very few people knew of our actions—and we were perfectly happy to have these issues discussed and resolved internally, without public embarrassment.

Title IX and Women's Athletics

Another important issue related to women's athletics. As a member of the House Higher Education Committee, which meant overseeing the budget and activities of our state's university system, I learned that women athletes on our college campuses did not have their own athletics programs, much less their own athletics director.

Title IX of the June 1972 federal Education Amendments prohibited discrimination against girls and women in federally funded education, including athletics programs. The provision was co-authored by two Democrats: Hawaii's Representative Patsy Mink and Oregon's Representative Edith Green. But national legislation has no effect locally until it is implemented at the state level, and Hawaii was not in compliance. My work on equal rights at both the local and national levels made paramount the task of addressing Title IX inequities in my home state.

I convinced my colleagues on the committee that women deserved their own leadership, their own facilities and certainly their own funding. I put the University of Hawaii on notice that I intended to make this subject one of my very highest priorities.

This made the administrators and constituents of the men's athletics programs—including Paul Durham, UH athletics director from 1968 to 1975,[26] and his successor, Ray Nagel[27]—very nervous. Many feared that elevating opportunities and funding for women athletes could put funding of the men's programs in jeopardy.

Fortunately, my fellow legislators on both the higher education and budget committees acknowledged the discrimination and found a solution. The law we passed created—and provided the necessary funding for—a separate women's athletics program with its own director.

Donnis Thompson became the first women's athletic director at UH in 1972. Under her leadership, several women's sports teams—including volleyball and golf—achieved the kind of attention both locally and nationally that draws fans and additional revenue, which more than paid for the women's athletics program.[28] The 1982 and 1983 Rainbow Wahine volleyball teams, under head coach Dave Shoji, went 67–3, becoming the first program in NCAA women's volleyball history to win consecutive national titles.[29]

A Family Legacy Comes Full Circle

During my second term as a state representative, I had one of the greatest surprises of my life. It had nothing to do with my political involvement, although being active in the community must have caught attention.

Henry Walker paid me an unexpected visit and presented me with an offer I couldn't refuse. He invited me to sit on the board of directors at Amfac, where he was president and CEO.[30] I was flabbergasted! Never before had any woman sat on any board at any of the Big Five companies in Hawaii. These five corporations—Alexander & Baldwin, American Factors, C. Brewer, Castle & Cooke and Theo. H. Davies—were the most powerful and successful corporations in our state.

Walker felt strongly that women should be represented in the business world in Hawaii. It was certainly not a token appointment; he asked me to serve as an officer in charge of personnel.

In my state of shock, I told him I would have to consult my father, Kazuo Fukuda, before accepting. My father, then a longtime employee of Amfac at its Hilo branch, couldn't believe that his daughter had been asked to sit on the board of the company where he worked. He was both proud and embarrassed that I had postponed accepting this honor until I had consulted him. Walker, however, thought it respectful and considerate of me to honor my father before accepting this new challenge.

My appointment was approved at a special meeting of shareholders on August 30, 1972. Soon after came a request to sit on the board of Hawaiian Airlines, where Mr. John H. "Jack" Magoon,[31] its president and majority owner, also was a pioneer in recruiting women.[32]

That September, I appeared with a panel of business leaders during a live television broadcast on KGMB-TV Channel 9.[33] The moderator bluntly asked me, "How can you in good conscience be a state representative and also be a director of a local airline [*sic*] without subscribing to a conflict of interest?" The *Honolulu Star-Bulletin* documented my response in an article published Friday, September 9: "If you view the state government as a super dooper [*sic*] business, I think it's incumbent on me to learn how business works." I promised that I would not let my business interests interfere with my judgment in legislative matters and would excuse myself from voting on any measure that could present a conflict.

Hawaii's Own Medical and Law Schools

As a member of the Senate Higher Education Committee, I joined with Democrat Committee chair Senator Francis Wong to examine the possible creation of a four-year medical school at the University of Hawaii. We had a powerful ally in Governor Burns, who originally had the dream of such a school to provide for the medical needs of our community.

I had a personal reason for getting involved. Hawaii students interested in medicine as a career often were forced to change their residency to a state where a medical school existed before they could seek admission there. Even then, there was no assurance the school would accept them. Temple University, a public research university in Philadelphia, and Hahnemann Medical College[34] were among the coveted options, and competition for enrollment was fierce.

For Hawaii students, access to home-based medical education had taken a step forward in 1965 when the University of Hawaii introduced a two-year medical school on campus. It made no sense to me that we still, five years later, had to send our students off-island so they could finish becoming doctors. Training them locally would be more cost effective for the students and would elevate the standard of health care here at home.

Governor Burns was a far-sighted visionary and had been first to propose a home-based, four-year medical school.[35] He had asked the Army to trade property that was once part of its coastal defense plan[36] to keep Mount Leahi at Diamond Head as a possible site, with Leahi Hospital as a training hospital for students.

As an aside, let me share a little about my relationship with Governor Burns.

In 1970, as a fairly new member of the legislature, and while following an old custom of leaning over the railings at the state capitol, I felt a tug on my arm. It was the governor. He said he wanted me to work hard and do well for our state, which needed thoughtful and effective Republicans. "That way," he said, "my guys can be kept honest."

That day, we shared some thoughts of a future Hawaii. He offered to help in my district, should I need it. I immediately took him up on it. I was concerned about children I saw swinging their legs over the rails of a pedestrian bridge spanning the freeway to Waialae School. I asked that additional barriers be installed to prevent this dangerous habit. The governor was good to his word. It was done the next day.

Unfortunately, the governor couldn't work the same magic with the legislature, which failed to act on his dream of a four-year medical school. The property at Diamond Head remained vacant.

During my time in the House, hope remained for a full-fledged, four-year medical school. As it happened, there were those in the Senate who wanted a law school. A compromise took place: It was decided we would work together toward a four-year medical school *and* a law school. It took skillful planning, but what was thought impossible happened and both schools opened in 1973.

The medical school, headed by Dean Terry Rogers, remained on campus, so Governor Burns's dream of locating it on Mount Leahi did not materialize, but the John A. Burns School of Medicine—known as JABSOM, and located adjacent to Kakaako Waterfront Park near downtown Honolulu—did. It accepts about 70 new medical students each year, many from underrepresented backgrounds and underserved areas in Hawaii and the Pacific Basin.[37]

The property at Diamond Head would later be put to good use.

Western Interstate Commission on Higher Education

Medicine wasn't the only field in which local students lacked opportunities to undertake professional education and training. Many other professions—including veterinary medicine, optometry, pharmacology and physical therapy—required off-island study and certification. After our success in achieving a local medical school, I felt a strong need to address these deficits. My near-term solution was to seek the cooperation of legislatures in states that already had these professional schools. In exchange, we could offer opportunities in other fields—forestry, marine biology, astronomy and others—their states did not provide.

In 1973, Governor Burns, who knew of my passion for higher education for our young people, appointed me to the Western Interstate Commission on Higher Education (WICHE). This pact of 13 western states [38] agreed, through acts by their legislatures and governors, to allow qualified students in these states to matriculate in their areas of interest to member-state universities at in-state tuition rates. The state legislatures in the pact funded the associated budget requirement, opening many opportunities for our young people.

In 1977, George Ariyoshi, who succeeded Burns as governor in October 1973, was chairman of the Western Governors Association and a supporter of the WICHE program. He appointed me to a second term as commissioner; I was subsequently elected chair. In total, I served as a commissioner of WICHE for eight years and had the privilege of serving as its chair for an unprecedented two terms, from 1978 through 1980.

It was during Governor Ariyoshi's tenure that questions arose in some state legislatures as to whether they could commit to continued participation in the reciprocal postsecondary education program. I remember working closely with Governor Ariyoshi to retain these states' confidence in the program, which had helped so many young people affordably achieve professional careers. He reached out to gain support from the governors of the states involved; I traveled to visit the various state legislatures. Our efforts kept the pact in place. The program continues today with a commitment to collaborations that provide educational opportunities for all young people.

Building the Party

In 1971, during my second term in the House, I held a leadership role as assistant minority floor leader and worked closely with Representative Andrew Poepoe, who held the same position. We monitored legislation and spoke on the floor on behalf of our party minority group. We also shared hopes of growing our caucus, which then numbered 17, by electing more Republicans to office.

In 1973, when our caucus had dropped to 16 (representing just 29 percent of the 55 available seats), we embarked on what we called a "targeting effort" to research and identify candidates to run in areas where we thought Republicans could win. We attempted to convince party leaders that this more scientific and practical approach to choosing and preparing qualified candidates would win elections and result in better representation from our party. When our attempt to persuade them fell flat, we decided to take our idea to a different audience.

We found some true believers in businessmen like Henry Walker, head of Amfac, and Malcom MacNaughton, head of Castle & Cooke.[39] They raised $350,000, which was big money in the 1970s, to fund our recruiting effort. We hired a Los Angeles political consulting firm headed by George Young, who was known for his success with California governor Ronald Reagan's 1970 reelection campaign.[40]

George brought with him a contingent of young, eager professionals who knew the ins and outs of campaigning, including fundraising. They included Anne Stanley, who later would become a member of my state Senate staff.[41]

Some of the other campaign trainers included Doug Eagleson, who later started a small business of his own; Ralph Sewald, who stayed in Hawaii and worked on other local Republican campaigns; and Paul Sullivan, who finished law school and practiced in Washington, D.C., Staffer Lucia Poepoe and Ann Orr, our photographer, also made significant contributions.

With the help of local Republican loyalists such as Dr. Franklin Kometani and his volunteers, we analyzed the various districts and sought individuals within those areas who were eager to run for office. It was a disciplined effort. Each candidate was assigned a proven campaign strategist to support and inform their development as an effective politician. Mentors counseled candidates on everything from tactics to fundraising to preparation for media appearances and public speaking. We covered all efforts necessary to winning a campaign.

Our targeting program paid off. That fall, we elected six new members to the state House of Representatives. Democrat Tadao Beppu, then Speaker of the House, was defeated by Dan Hakoda, one of our freshly minted candidates. Other first-timers included Donna Ikeda of Hawaii Kai, Faith Evans from the windward side of Oahu and Richard "Ike" Sutton, a Pearl Harbor survivor who represented Nuuanu. No seats were lost that election season; the six newly elected representatives helped maintain our total of 16 Republicans in the state House.

Our experiment had proven successful, but much to our frustration, the local party establishment did not support continuing the program.

From House to Senate

After six years in the state House, I decided to run for the state Senate. The campaign would not be easy. I had to unseat a good friend and fellow Amfac board member: Kenneth Brown, who was well known in the business and Native Hawaiian communities.

Again, my family played pivotal roles in this campaign. My parents came from Hilo to help—my mother to do the cooking and my father to walk the district with me. People in the neighborhoods were so taken with my father that they asked to meet him and "talk story." I'm sure he got more votes for me than I did.

My children were put to work holding signs on the highway. We got innovative and followed the example set by the Burma Shave product advertising popular in those years.[42] Our five children would line up, each one with a different sign: "please," "vote," "for," "our," "MOM"— and there I would be, last in line, with my name, "Pat Saiki," on my sign. The lineup caused so much distraction for drivers that we quickly discarded the approach for fear of causing auto accidents.

Nevertheless, we won peoples' attention, cementing my name recognition, and I was elected to represent the 7th Senatorial District, which encompassed two representative districts—the 8th and 9th. It was a multimember senate district, with four members. My colleagues were Donald Nishimura and Dennis O'Connor, both Democrats, and fellow Republican Fred Rohlfing.

Our district covered the areas from Palolo to St. Louis Heights to Hawaii Kai. My entry in the 25-member state Senate made me part of a small cadre of four women—Mary George, a fellow Republican, came from the Honolulu City Council, and Democrats Jean King and Patsy Young joined me in moving from the House to the Senate.

Now I sat as a member of both the Higher and Lower Education Committees, with a chance to address many of the Department of

Education policies I had objected to when I was a schoolteacher.

During this time, I saw an opportunity to strengthen employee-bargaining power for Hawaii teachers. The Teacher's Chapter of the Hawaii Government Employees Association, which I'd helped initiate in the mid-1960s, was purely local. Now I pushed to dissolve that organization, urging members to instead join national unions based in Washington, D.C., This came as quite a shock to many people, but I knew it was the right thing to do. It would give our teachers a stronger voice and representation in national discussions. Teachers today can be members of the Hawaii State Teachers Association, an affiliate of the National Education Association, or the Hawaii Federation of Teachers, an affiliate of the American Federation of Teachers.

Sex Abuse Treatment Center

One evening when I returned home from a day at the legislature, my husband, who always took great interest in and supported my work, shared some deeply troubling news. Stanley, who was then chief of staff at Kapiolani Hospital, told me that women who had been raped or had suffered abuse were being taken by police to the county morgue, of all places, for an examination by a physician. This was an established procedure! It's no wonder women were hesitant to make charges against their perpetrators. (These hesitancies exist even today. Women are often questioned not as victims, but as instigators of the crime.)

Stanley felt the conditions suffered by these women bordered on inhumane.

There was no reason a woman who had suffered such trauma could not be in a hospital setting, attended by sympathetic nurses and doctors. Stanley sought the support of Richard Davi, CEO and administrator of Kapiolani Hospital,[43] to provide a more logical and humane setting and approach: a hospital-based sex abuse treatment center.

All my husband needed was funding to provide this service. I offered to see what could be done to legislate and fund such an entity. I faced few arguments from my colleagues in the legislature after approaching them on a personal basis and asking, "If this unthinkable crime had happened to your daughter, aunt, sister or even your mother, would you not want them to have the proper professional attention they deserved?" The bill received unanimous approval and funding was approved.

The Sex Abuse Treatment Center opened in 1976 to provide 24-hour crisis and legal support services for victims and their families.[44] Staff developed protocols for medical examinations and evidence collection for sexual assault crimes.

Counseling services were provided to victims and their families. Medical personnel, police and prosecutors were trained on victim sensitivity.

With this level of support, victims were more willing to report sexual assault to the police and testify in court. They were also better able to recover from trauma.

Under Adriana Ramelli, the center's effective executive director for 36 years, the center has developed and also expanded its role to meet the needs of the abused victims of sex trafficking statewide. In 2018, the center celebrated its 40th anniversary.

Leveling the Playing Field for Homeowners

During this time, I also saw an opportunity to correct a longstanding discriminatory practice that allowed landowners to dictate who could lease or purchase their property. My family's experience trying to buy a home in Aina Haina was an example of that injustice, and a reminder that the law had to be changed to allow homeownership for all, regardless of race or ethnicity.

In 1975, my Republican colleague Senator Fred Rohlfing championed a bill that eventually became Act 184–Relating to Residential Leaseholds, which I supported and worked to pass, along with 19 of the 28 senators.[45] It pointed out that in Oahu alone there were 72 major landowners (mostly estates) controlling 72.5 percent of available land. The bill outlined all the conditions under which leasehold rentals can be sold as "fee simple."

The leasehold land system required homeowners to pay landowners for the right to live on the land. There was a benefit to this form of land ownership—it generally kept prices lower for homes built upon leasehold land. That's because the value of the property wasn't factored into the price of the actual house.

Land has particular value on islands, where it is a desirable and finite resource. But there was a significant downside for homeowners, who faced uncertainty after their lease ran out, typically after 30 years. Homeowners had none of the long-term security usually associated with home ownership.

Many communities were "leasehold rental" households that gathered together to form negotiation teams to bargain for ownership. Most were successful. Many of the large estates were broken up and more secure home ownership became the norm. It was most satisfying to see that through these efforts, racial discrimination under the constitution no longer existed, and homeownership prevailed.

China Makes an Impression

For 30 years after the founding of the People's Republic of China in 1949 the United States did not formally recognize its authority, choosing instead to maintain diplomatic relations with the Republic of China government on Taiwan. Travel to China was prohibited until President Richard M. Nixon lifted the travel ban in March of 1971.[46]

So, it was quite an honor to be invited, along with 17 other women selected from throughout the country, to represent the United States during a three-week work-study visit to China.

Our delegation arrived on October 4, 1975, to study the business, economic, educational and cultural aspects of China. We were guests of the China Friendship Association and sponsored by the American Women for International Understanding.[47] The tour took us to seven cities: Guangzhou (formerly Canton),[48] Guilin (formerly Kweilin),[49] Shanghai, Hangzhou (Hangchow),[50] Nanjing (Nanking), Xian (Sian)[51] and Peking (now Beijing).

My colleagues were impressive. They included Virginia Knauer, special assistant to President Gerald R. Ford for consumer affairs;[52] Helen W. Miliken, First Lady of Michigan;[53] and Elly M. Petersen, member of the president's Consumer Advisory Council. My roommate was Congresswoman Edith Green of Oregon,[54] a Democrat, who had co-authored Title IX with U.S. Representative Patsy Mink,[55] a Democrat from Hawaii. I was the only state legislator on the trip and was appointed by President Nixon.

We visited banks, hydroelectric plants, communes, textile tool-and-dye factories, hospitals and schools. Despite what we'd heard about China oppressing its people, we were impressed to see women being educated, participating in business and moving in the direction of equality. I guess they wanted to show us that since the rise of Chairman Mao, women were being treated respectfully.

My interests and concerns involved the education of young children in China. I was surprised to learn that there was still much government control over the upbringing of young people. At 56 days after birth, children were placed in nursery schools, where they stayed until the age of six. Children were promoted to primary school, then to middle school, which they attended until the age of 18. At that point, most were deployed to a farm or a factory. All had to learn another language as early as the fourth grade. Most selected English, which was favored by Chairman Mao.

Only the most talented students were allowed to further their studies at a technical school or institution of higher learning. Only these students were allowed to choose their professions. The strict governmental control over young children and the trajectory of their lives came as a shock to me.

Most of the women we saw were still confined to olive "Mao jackets" and loose-fitting trousers. None used makeup or cosmetics. We had anticipated that. Before leaving the U.S., we asked cosmetic giants Revlon, Max Factor and Proctor & Gamble to contribute makeup kits including lipstick, rouge and face powder.

Wherever we went, we quietly handed these "goodies" to the ladies. They loved the gifts and lifetime friends were made.

We moved through the country in a caravan of cars (Mercedes-Benz, no less), with one of us in the back seat and a tour guide in the front seat. We were careful in choosing topics of conversation; we knew that every evening the guides would undergo "debriefing" sessions where they would repeat our conversations to government officials.

We ended our work-study tour in Beijing, where George H. W. Bush and his wife, Barbara, hosted us during a memorable evening. Then ambassador to the United Nations,[56] George Bush was in China as a special envoy of the United States. But the main reason I call the visit memorable is because it was the first time in three weeks that we enjoyed fresh, raw vegetables in a salad—vegetables grown in the Bush compound—and drank fresh, safe water. To be safe on the road we had to choose between canned beer and fruit juices. I remember Barbara Bush showing us a wall hanging she was quilting. I saw the same quilt on the wall of the White House when George H. W. Bush became president of the U.S.

At the conclusion to our trip to China, we were hosted to a formal dinner in the Great Hall of China by the First Lady, Madame Jiang Qing (Mrs. Mao). It was most impressive.

Emergency Medical Services Act

As a member of the Senate Health Committee, I had an ally in its chairman, Senator Donald D. H. Ching. He was a dedicated man committed to bettering the health of our people. He greatly respected my husband as a fellow member of the board of directors for the Hawaii Medical Services Association. It was with a hopeful attitude that I brought to his attention one of my husband's greatest concerns.

The Emergency Medical Services department run by the City & County of Honolulu was based on a model designed by the Hawaii Medical Association.

It operated well enough on Oahu as a "scoop and run" ambulance service, offering simple first aid and transport to the hospital,[57] but the Neighbor Islands had to rely on fire departments for emergency medical transportation to local hospitals.

Stanley envisioned a statewide system offering comprehensive emergency medical services by highly trained personnel with access to equipment that allowed them to communicate in real time with hospital emergency departments.

Programs were needed at our university to train paramedics, or emergency medical technicians, and specialists called mobile intensive care technicians. Creating and funding these professional programs would ensure quality care was accessible to all citizens in our state, no matter where they lived.

Many HMA member doctors—including Dr. Herbert Chinn, one of our state's first urologists;[58] Dr. Livingston Wong, who pioneered kidney and bone marrow transplants in Hawaii;[59] and Dr. Douglas Ostman, an emergency medicine specialist—shared this vision and worked to bring it about.

The idea of coordinated emergency medical training was enthusiastically supported by legislators from the Big Island, Maui and Kauai. What we needed was a statewide program written into law.

I was encouraged when Senator Ching shared my concern and recognized the urgency of tackling this task. He offered his help and gave me a three-day deadline to write a state law to encompass all the necessities—education, training, implementation, coordination with Neighbor Island needs and funding. I gathered together all the knowledgeable people I could find, including the HMA medical experts, HMA executive director Jon Won and his assistant Becky Kendro, lawyers from the Legislative Reference Bureau and Dr. Wong's wife, Linda Wright Wong, who did a lot of legwork. Jose Lee, a longtime trusted staff member, was in constant touch with Hawaii Supreme Court justice Kazuhisa Abe, HMA's legislative legal counsel, who offered consultation and advice on its behalf. Input from Ralph Goto, coordinator of the City & County Department of Ocean Safety, ensured emergency services would include assistance to those affected by ocean incidents.

We all got to work, 24/7 for some of us, including my husband. I still find it amazing that we accomplished this by or before the deadline and were able to present a comprehensive piece of legislation to the committee. It received unanimous support and we got it done. Act 148, Session Laws of Hawaii passed both the House and Senate and was signed into law in 1978 by Governor Ariyoshi.

This was, by far, one of my most satisfying experiences as a lawmaker.

My sense of accomplishment was dampened only slightly by Chairman Ching's reluctance to include me in acknowledging the players behind this extraordinary effort.

"Without mentioning any names," Senator Ching announced, as the Statewide Emergency Medical Services Act passed on April 15, "I must congratulate a woman minority senator. … I won't mention any names, but she knows who I'm talking about."[60]

The "Strange Coalition"

When 1981 rolled around, an eruption occurred in the state Senate. In the run-up to the legislative session, a major fissure separated the group of eight that supported former Senate president John Ushijima and the group of nine that backed incumbent Senate president Richard "Dickie" Wong. The Ushijima group included George Toyofuku, Dennis O'Connor, Charles Campbell, Milton Holt, Norman Mizuguchi and Gerald Machida. They wanted to wrest the Senate presidency back to Ushijima. Battle lines were drawn, dividing the Democrat majority.

The Wong group included Ben Cayetano, Neil Abercrombie, Duke Kawasaki, Steve Cobb, Clifford Uwaine, Dante Carpenter, Joseph Kuroda, Patsy Young and Mamoru Yamasaki. Their strategy to retain power depended on the willingness of eight Republicans to form a coalition with them.

Our Republican leader, Senator D. G. "Andy" Anderson, engaged in intense negotiations with both groups of Democrats. Republicans approached included me and senators Wadsworth Yee, Richard Henderson, Ralph Ajifu, Mary George, Ann Kobayashi and Buddy Soares.

The warring Democrat factions needed the support of all eight of us to win.

We ended up working with the Wong faction.

The resultant arrangement was editorialized in the press as "a Strange Coalition in the State Senate." It was seen as a marriage of convenience between the very "liberal" Wong group and the more "conservative" Republican group led by Senator Anderson.

Andy insisted that we Republicans hold committee chairmanships in the Senate. This precipitated problems. Wong supporter Senator Neil Abercrombie was chair of the Higher Education Committee, on which I sat. I questioned Neil's leadership—most significantly, I did not agree with the direction he wanted to take the University of Hawaii. For example, Neil and his cronies wanted to locate Kapiolani Community College (which is part of the University of Hawaii system) in an urban McCully neighborhood high-rise. This would have been disastrous—I didn't think a community college belonged in a high-rise!

I felt my being chair of this committee was essential to progress in our university system. It took a crucial three days to convince Neil to step down and agree to take the chairmanship of the K–12 education committee. Andy made the most of his negotiating advantage and it was his firm leadership that led to the "strange coalition" with the Wong group. The understanding was that our policy differences would be aired and respected.

Wong was reelected president of the Senate. We Republicans gained an unprecedented six committee chairmanships and considerable memberships on key committees.[61] And I learned an important lesson: When you are in a position to influence the balance of power, you must be willing to extract the best for your colleagues.

I was delighted to learn that I would chair the Senate Committee on Higher Education. The moment I assumed the position, I called Dr. Fujio Matsuda, president of the University of Hawaii. Dr. Matsuda had been under assault by Neil Abercrombie, who was calling for his resignation after a questionable audit. Imagine his excitement when he heard I'd replaced Abercrombie.

To get things moving in a positive direction, I urged Dr. Matsuda to get a yellow bulldozer sent to Mount Leahi[62] that very day, to signal to all the new location of Kapiolani Community College. He strongly endorsed the move.

Dr. Matsuda was one of the more outstanding UH presidents. He served from 1974 to 1985 with foresight and a good sense of planning. His assistant, Harold Masumoto, was enormously capable in his own right and later became vice president of administration at the university. We at the legislature, especially those of us on the Committee on Higher Education, were constantly in touch with Harold to learn of the administration's thinking on university matters. He and Dr. Matsuda worked very effectively as a team.

Another person important to implement this preferred plan was Dr. Joyce Tsunoda, then provost of KCC, who also heartily endorsed the new Mount Leahi location. She gathered her loyal assistants, including chief assistant Pat Snyder.

With the help of the UH engineers, planners and site specialists we put plans in place for the campus buildings, parking and infrastructure.

I instructed them to make sure the designs reflected the ambiance of the existing neighborhood—and that ample parking was available. I made them aware that my tenure as chair of Higher Education would last only two years, which meant essential progress must be made within that time. The people involved at the university to implement construction of this campus included Harold Masumoto, Robert Hara, engineer in charge of construction, and Robert Matsushita, chief architect. They met the basic deadlines and the foundations of the campus were well on the way when my tenure as chair ended.

Meanwhile, I gave priority to building the university's law school library. The University of Hawaii at Manoa William S. Richardson School of Law was located on the upper campus on a ridgeline with a dramatic view of Waikiki. My predecessor, Neil Abercrombie, following a suggestion from Senator Ben Cayetano, a Democrat representing Pearl City, sought to locate the library in a quarry—a deep pit located below the law school. That would require a set of steps going from the school down to the lower elevation of the library. The recommendation failed to take into account that it often rains in Manoa. Steps going down to the quarry location would be slippery, dangerous and unmanageable for many students, especially those with disabilities. To me, the idea was ridiculous.

There were other studies and new suggestions, including moving the law school library next to the law school on Dole Street. The challenge to find a suitable location was mine, and options were limited. Dr. Matsuda gave me some good suggestions and I personally drove to every possible site. I could only find one location next to the existing law school that would adequately ensure access and safety to the library. It was the only site that made sense, but it meant the loss of 15 parking spaces, which the administration found difficult to accept. I persuaded administrators to make the tough decision, arguing that the sacrifice of a few parking spaces would be worth it.

The "strange coalition" dissolved after two years, but I had made the most of my role as chair of Higher Education. It was most satisfying to see the Kapiolani Community College in its new home on Diamond Head, and to have the UH Law Library designated for construction next to the law school.

Legislative Reapportionment

It is my opinion that the legislative reapportionment decisions made in 1981 indelibly impacted our state legislature and the future of politics in Hawaii.

Federal legislation based on the 1964 Supreme Court case *Reynolds v. Sims* ruled that the electoral districts of state legislative chambers must be roughly equal in population.[63] It was one in a series of Warren Court cases that applied the principle of "one person, one vote" to U.S. legislative bodies.[64]

Hawaii, until that point, had state House and Senate legislative districts with multiple members. Being able to vote for more than one representative or senator meant voters could choose both a Republican and a Democrat—allowing for more nuanced voting decisions based on individual candidates rather than strict party allegiance. Under this plan, voters looked at their legislative candidates with an open mind to having both political parties represented in their districts.

For example, my state Senate District 7 covered four House districts, from Palolo and St. Louis Heights to Hawaii Kai. It allowed for four Senate seats. Given a choice of quality candidates from both parties, voters preferred to have two Democrats and two Republicans represent them. The Democrats were the dominant party statewide, but voters in practice expressed a preference for competing-party representation and a better balance of power.

That was the case when I ran for the state Senate in 1974. Four of us were elected from Senate District 7: Democrats Donald Nishimura and Dennis O'Connor and Republicans Fred Rohlfing and me.[65] The 1978 Senate election again saw four senators elected: Democrats Steve Cobb and Dennis O'Connor and Republicans Buddy Soares and me.[66] It was quite evident that voters believed representation from both parties was the best approach.

In 1981, a reapportionment took place (they take place every ten years) and the discussion of adhering strictly to "one man, one vote" by doing away with multimember districts took place at the state's new Reapportionment Commission.

Two commission representatives who happened to be members of the Republican Party—Carla Coray, the Republican national committeewoman, and Jim Hall, a party loyalist—agreed with the concept of "one man, one vote" but wanted to extend the concept to include single-member legislative districts in both the House and Senate. They lobbied mightily for this change.

I strongly disagreed and made it known to our representatives on the commission. Republicans were already in the minority. This measure would weaken opportunities for Republicans to get elected head-to-head against Democratic candidates, whose political dominance was rooted in ties to union leaders and members—state and county workers and their families who leaned Democrat to preserve their jobs.

I must acknowledge and respect Coray and Hall for their spirit of head-to-head battle in support of their strongly held beliefs. But I believed then, and continue to believe today, that such reapportionment bravado is not politically practical.

As I predicted, once Hawaii implemented single-member state legislative districts, the whole political spectrum changed. We Republicans handed full rein of the legislative process to the Democrats. The miserable results of that loss quickly became evident.

After the 1981 reapportionment went into effect, starting with the 1982 elections, the state Senate included eight Republicans out of 25 seats and the House had 12 out of 51. In 1983, the Senate had five Republicans and the House had seven. By 1986, there were only four Republicans in the Senate; the House had 11. In 2017, the state Senate lost *all* Republican representation (making Hawaii the only state in the nation without a single Republican state senator) and had just five Republicans in the state House of Representatives. Today we have just one Republican in the Senate and only five Republicans in the state House.

Many factors led to the diminishing numbers of Republicans in office, but the single-member district concept for both House and Senate seats did not make things easier for minority candidates.

New Directions

In 1982, Senator Andy Anderson decided to run for governor and invited me to join his ticket as lieutenant governor. It was a difficult decision. Should I give up a seat I enjoyed so much in the state Senate? Or should I take the risk on a greater challenge? Anderson was a proven, dynamic leader dedicated to improving our state. He was a successful businessman who built and ran John Dominis, one of Honolulu's most popular special-occasion restaurants, along with a host of other business ventures.[67] He had the political skills and executive experience to make a good governor. I decided to invest in the Anderson-Saiki ticket.

After a vigorous primary campaign, incumbent Democrat Governor George Ariyoshi overcame a challenge from Jean King, who had served with him as lieutenant governor. He announced John Waihee[68] as his new choice for lieutenant governor and the race was on.

Our campaign was a difficult one—we were up against a Japanese American incumbent who ran as the "quiet but effective" candidate, and who had not made any serious errors in his first term. He appealed to members of the conservative electorate, who preferred not to change the status quo. The Democrat Party was organized and funded and much support from established businesses and unions went to our opponents.

Our campaign was a courageous effort and Andy and I made a good team, but we were up against an ingrained Democrat constituency and it was not meant to be. We lost that race, but I learned valuable lessons.

Back to the Party

After the defeat, I felt even more convinced that if Hawaii were ever to have representation by both major political parties in our government, we had to build the Republican Party to be an opposition party of substance—a voice to make government more responsive to all people and to new ideas. I thought the helm of the Republican Party would be an exciting challenge and a means by which we could become a serious entity in Hawaii politics.

I sought the party chairmanship determined to awaken like-minded people to join in this effort. I ran, was elected and served for two terms—four years—during which we increased our membership, raised money to support candidates and began to grow into an entity to be respected.

We opened our headquarters in a downtown Honolulu office and I took on the mission to strengthen our party. With the help of steady supporters from Bishop Street, the heart of our big business community[69]—including Amfac president and CEO Henry Walker; Malcolm MacNaughton, president of Castle & Cooke; Jack Magoon, president of Hawaiian Airlines; and other prominent Republican businessmen—we had a steady financial source for party building and candidate support.

Volunteer supporters were vital to our success. I must also recognize a staff person who for many years served selflessly as our in-house administrator: Alice Hakikawa, who was always there to coordinate our activities while answering the phone, checking the mail and taking messages. We could always count on Alice, who was dedicated to our party and its mission. We could never pay her what she deserved, but we made sure to provide her with basic retirement benefits so she could enjoy her eventual golden years. We will never forget her!

In two and a half years as party chair, and with the help of an active state committee, we expanded our membership threefold and raised more than $800,000. We increased our numbers from seven to 11 in the House, but lost one Senate seat, ending up with four Republican senators. Still, that was significant progress in this Democrat state.

With the party finances and structure in better shape and active new leaders involved to carry on, I turned my attention back to elective politics.

On opening day at the state legislature, Pat sits at her desk with her mentor and friend, Henry Walker, president and chief executive officer of Amfac, Inc. Pat's mother, Shizue Fukuda, sits behind her.

A VOTE FOR
PAT SAIKI
MEANS ACTION

ENVIRONMENT

"We must plan for tomorrow so that our children may continue to enjoy the natural beauties of Hawaii."

TAXES

"Hawaii will be facing a tax increase next year . . . unless government spending is brought under control."

TRAFFIC

"Solutions must be found to relieve traffic congestion . . . mass transit systems are the only alternative."

CRIME

"Too many of our homes have been burglarized and vandalized. Our homes must be protected through strong enforcement of our criminal laws."

EDUCATION

"We have come a long way in providing our children with sound education. As a member of the House Education Committee, I have worked for further improvement to guarantee our children the tools necessary to become productive members of our complex society."

Re-Elect
REP. PATRICIA (PAT) SAIKI
STATE HOUSE OF REPRESENTATIVES
NINTH DISTRICT ®

PAT SAIKI
PAT SAIKI
PAT SAIKI
PAT SAIKI
PAT SAIKI
PAT SAIKI

GOOD FRIENDS OF **PAT SAIKI**

PAID FOR BY
Raymond M. Torkildson
Franklin Kometani
co-chairmen

784 Elepaio St.
Honolulu, Hawaii 96816
Phone: 734-0200

Re-Elect
PAT SAIKI

REPRESENTATIVE
PATRICIA SAIKI
Assistant Minority Floor Leader

fOR the past four years, **PAT SAIKI** has served the people of our district as a "full time" Representative in the State House. Pat's colleagues elected her their Assistant Minority Floor Leader. Her persistant efforts to pass good legislation were recognized by the Eagleton Institute of Politics of Rutgers University, which named her one of the "most promising legislators". Furthermore, the National Society of State Legislators has asked **PAT SAIKI** to join their Board of Governors.

President Nixon, in seeking a spokesman for Hawaii, appointed **PAT SAIKI** to his Advisory Council on the Status of Women.

In 1968, Pat, as a delegate to the Constitutional Convention, participated in molding our State Constitution which is considered one of the finest in the nation.

In addition to her legislative responsibilities, **PAT SAIKI** has continued her involvement in community activities. She now serves as chairman of the Hawaii Special Olympics for mentally retarded children and the Heart Sunday Drive. As chairman of the Kalani Band Boosters, Pat helped send our youngsters to the Sun and Sugar Bowl parades. The Junior League chose Pat for its Community Advisory Board.

PAT SAIKI graduated from Hilo High and the UH, and for 12 years taught at Punahou, Kaimuki Intermediate and Kalani High. Pat, her husband, Dr. Stanley M. Saiki, and their five children live at 784 Elepaio St.

Pat stands in front of her office door at the state House of Representatives at the then-new state capitol.

Opposite page: *One of Pat's campaign brochures for the 1972 election, when she successfully sought reelection to the state House of Representatives.*

Pat, standing at front row, far left, was one of the women invited to visit China in 1975. She was the only state legislator in the group.

State Representative Pat Saiki on the floor of the House of Representatives with Republican Representatives Andy Poepoe and Hiram Fong Jr.

Pat at the opening of the state legislature with the president and CEO of Hawaiian Airlines, John "Jack" Magoon.

*Pat ran for lieutenant governor on the Republican ticket in 1982
with gubernatorial candidate D. G. "Andy" Anderson.*

PART II ENDNOTES

1   "During the first half of the 20th century, the Republican Party dominated Hawaii politics. In the 1956 elections the Democrats, gaining strength from labour unions and from returning World War II Japanese American veterans, surged to power. The Democrats won the governorship in 1962 and held it until 2002, and they have been dominant in state legislative elections and in federal elections." https://www.britannica.com/place/Hawaii-state/Cultural-life

2   Tom Coffman, Catch a Wave: A Case Study of Hawaii's New Politics (Honolulu: Star-Bulletin Printing Co., 1972), 203.

3   "First Women to Serve in State and Territorial Legislatures," NCSL.org, National Conference of State Legislatures, http://www.ncsl.org/legislators-staff/legislators/womens-legislative-network/first-women-in-state-legislatures.aspx.

4   "Interview with Momi Min," Juniroa Productions, August 27, 2014, video, 22:23, http://uluulu.hawaii.edu/titles/5230.

5   *Honolulu Star-Bulletin* staff-written obituary (undated): https://www.newspapers.com/clip/23117212/sarah_pule_obit/

6   Forbes was the only female state senator from either party from 1967 until she retired in 1974. James V. Hall, "Hawaii's history is full of female GOP trailblazers," *Honolulu* Magazine, November 28, 2004, http://archives.starbulletin.com/2004/11/28/editorial/commentary.html. or 6. James V. Hall, "Hawaii's history is full of female GOP trailblazers," *Star-Bulletin*, November 28, 2004, http://archives.starbulletin.com/2004/11/28/editorial/commentary.html.

7   "The State of Hawaii: 55 Years of Statehood—A Legislative History," August 21, 1959 to 2014, Photo Composites and Member Listing 1959 through 2014: https://www.capitol.hawaii.gov/session2014/docs/House-YearBook.pdf

8   Raymond M. Torkildson was a lawyer with Torkildson, Katz, Moore and Hetherington, and an Army major who served in World War II. http://archives.starbulletin.com/2007/12/21/news/obits.html

9   Alexander James Napier was born on Maui, the son of a Scotsman who landed in Hawaii in 1912 with a shipment of cattle from Missouri. A second-generation rancher, he became politically active to better the ranching and livestock industry in Hawaii. https://www.hicattle.org/paniolo-hall-of-fame/inductees/alexander-james-napier

10 "Advisory Council of Women Named; Nixon Chooses New Panel of 20 to Check on Status," *The New York Times*, August 17, 1969, https://www.nytimes.com/1969/08/17/archives/advisory-council-of-women-named-nixon-chooses-new-panel-of-20-to.html.

11 The fight for gender equality was first introduced as the Equal Rights Amendment by Alice Paul in 1923. https://www.equalrightsamendment.org/history

12 "His faith played a role in the toughest public policy issue of his Senate career, a bill that ended a century-old law that allowed abortion only to save the life of the mother. The bill, which made abortion a decision between a woman and her doctor, gained national attention since it was thought at the time to be the most permissive in the country. Yano, as chairman of the Senate Public Health Committee, initially held up progress on liberalizing the abortion law but eventually supported an outright repeal. 'After much reading and soul-searching, I am personally moving strongly towards the position that the present law should be repealed and abortion should not be a matter of legislation

but a question of conscience between mother and doctor,' he said." http://the.honolulu-advertiser.com/article/2005/Jun/10/ln/ln49p.html

13 "Bill to Legalize Abortions Clears Hawaii Legislature," *The New York Times*, February 25, 1970, https://www.nytimes.com/1970/02/25/archives/bill-to-legalize-abortions-clears-hawaii-legislature-bill-on.html.

14 "Hawaii this week becomes the first state in the Union to legalize abortion on request, leaving the decision about the operation to the woman herself and her physician. The legislature completed passage of the bill last week and sent it to Governor John A. Burns. A Roman Catholic, Burns said he would not sign it but neither would he veto it. Unsigned, it becomes law in ten days." "Medicine: Abortion on Request," *Time* magazine, March 9, 1970, http://content.time.com/time/subscriber/article/0,33009,878789,00.html.

15 https://www.kometaniassociates.com/our-team.html

16 Forbes was the only female state senator from either party from 1967 until she retired in 1974. James V. Hall, "Hawaii's history is full of female GOP trailblazers," Star-Bulletin, November 28, 2004, http://archives.starbulletin.com/2004/11/28/editorial/commentary.html.

17 "the woman's right [*sic*]," *Honolulu Advertiser*, Thursday, January 27, 1972.

18 "A Little Legal House Cleaning," Barbara Morgan, assistant women's editor, *Honolulu Advertiser* "Family Today" section, Friday, January 28, 1972:

19 "it's [*sic*] equal rights for this session with Patsy [*sic*] Saiki," *Honolulu Advertiser*, Wednesday, January 26, 1972

20 Congressional Record 117 (October 12, 1971) p. 35815.

21 "By 1977, the legislatures of 35 states had approved the amendment. In 1978, Congress voted to extend the original March 1979 deadline to June 30, 1982. However, no additional states voted yes before that date, and the ERA fell three states short of ratification." https://www.equalrightsamendment.org/era-ratification-map

22 Erika Engle, "Henry A. Walker: One of the last 'Big 5'," Pacific Business News, April 23, 2000, https://www.bizjournals.com/pacific/stories/2000/04/24/story5.html. Lori Tighe, "Henry Walker dies at 78," *Honolulu Star-Bulletin*, April 15, 2000, http://archives.starbulletin.com/2000/04/15/news/story2.html.

23 "At its peak, Liberty House had 45 to 50 stores with about 4,200 employees. After the company emerged from bankruptcy, Macy's took over the department store chain in 2001." Lisa Kubota, "18 years ago, Liberty House closed. For former employees, it seems like yesterday," Hawaii News Now, August 12, 2019, https://www.hawaiinewsnow.com/2019/08/13/years-later-employees-liberty-house-reunite-reflect-time-together/.

24 Waialae Country Club: https://waialaecc.com/web/pages/the-clubhouse.

25 Pacific Club: https://www.thepacificclub.org/Default.aspx?p=DynamicModule&page-id=407577&ssid=334595&vnf=1.

26 UH Hall of Fame: https://hawaiiathletics.com/hof.aspx?hof=16.

27 Ray Nagel was UH athletics director from 1976 to 1983. Dave Reardon, "Former UH athletic director Ray Nagel dies," *Honolulu Star-Advertiser*, January 21, 2015, https://www.staradvertiser.com/2015/01/21/sports/former-uh-athletic-director-ray-nagel-dies/.

28 Thompson was UH's first women's track and field coach and oversaw the commencement and growth of the women's intercollegiate athletics program as its first athletic director. Dr. Thompson arrived in Manoa to start the women's track and field program in 1961. Thompson gained national prominence when she guided the U.S. women's track team in competition against Russia and Poland in 1962. She coached the team for three years and returned to the Islands, after receiving her doctorate of education degree, to head the women's athletics program in 1972, the year Title IX began, and served in that capacity until 1981. She left UH in 1981 to become Hawaii's first woman superintendent of education. https://hawaiiathletics.com/news/2009/2/2/GEN_0202095128.aspx

29 Rainbow Wahine volleyball: https://hawaiiathletics.com/honors/hall-of-fame/1982-83-rainbow-wahine-volleyballteam/98.

30 *Hawaii Tribune-Herald*, July 30, 1972: "Mrs. Stanley (Patricia) Saiki, State House representative, and Mrs. Walter S. (Ellen Magnin) Newman of San Francisco will be nominated for election to the board of directors of Amfac, Inc., at a special meeting of shareholders August 30 in Honolulu. Walker said: 'Mrs. Saiki had a distinguished career as a teacher before entering public life as an elected member of the Hawaii State House of Representatives. She is accorded wide respect by members of both political parties in Honolulu and is a vigorous exponent of her independent ideas." The clip also says Pat was at that time serving as assistant minority floor leader at the state House, that she was selected the Most Promising Legislator of 1970 by the Eagleton Institute of Politics at Rutgers University and that she was a member of "President Nixon's Citizens Council on the Status of women [*sic*]."

31 "John H. Magoon, 87, Hawaiian Air Owner," *The New York Times*, November 26, 2003, https://www.nytimes.com/2003/11/26/business/john-h-magoon-87-hawaiian-air-owner.html.

32 Pat served on both boards for a total of 13 years, until her election to the U.S. Congress in 1986.

33 The panel included Herbert Cornuelle, president, Dillingham Corporation; Malcolm MacNaughton, board chair, Castle & Cooke, Inc.; Frank Manaut, president, Bank of Hawaii; Lawrence Pricher, president, Alexander & Baldwin, Inc.; and Edwin N. Wong, board chair, Chamber of Commerce of Hawaii.

34 Hahnemann Medical College became part of Drexel University College of Medicine in Philadelphia but eventually closed, in September 2019.

35 John A. Burns School of Medicine: https://jabsom.hawaii.edu/about-us/.

36 Fort Ruger: https://dod.hawaii.gov/hieng/files/2017/07/Addendum-1.pdf.

37 Diversity at JABSOM. https://jabsom.hawaii.edu/about-us/diversity-at-jabsom/.

38 WICHE is now comprised of 15 states.

39 Castle & Cooke did most of its business in agriculture, eventually becoming the Dole Food Company, the world's largest producer of fruits and vegetables. https://www.dole.com/aboutdole). In 1995 it was spun off from Dole and today most of the company's business is in real estate and residential, commercial and retail development. https://www.castlecookehawaii.com/Page/About-ALookBack).

40 Reelection campaign date verified: https://www.whitehouse.gov/about-the-white-house/presidents/ronald-reagan/.

41 After Pat left the state Senate, Ann went to work for the Republican National Committee in Washington, D.C. Pat was able to woo her back to serve as her chief of staff when she served as Administrator in the Small Business Administration from 1991 to 1993.

42 Burma-Shave was an American brand of brushless shaving cream famous for an advertising campaign featuring humorous (and sometimes morbid) rhyming poems on small sequential highway roadside signs. https://www.printmag.com/design-inspiration/the-morbid-roadside-ad-poetry-of-burma-shave/

43 Helen Alton, "Kapiolani health care visionary Richard Davi dies at 71," *Honolulu Star-Bulletin*, March 26, 1997, http://archives.starbulletin.com/97/03/26/community/obits.html.

44 Sex Abuse Treatment Center: http://satchawaii.com/about-satc/.

45 The bill was introduced and supported by a bipartisan group of senators including Patsy K. Young, Joseph T. Kuroda, T. C. Yim, Donald S. Nishimura, Donald H. Ching (majority leader), Robert S. Taira (majority floor leader), Anson Chong (assistant majority leader), Francis A. Wong (majority policy leader), D. G. Anderson (minority floor leader), Patricia Saiki, Henry Takitani, Richard S. H. Wong, George H. Toyofuki (assistant majority leader), Mary George, John Leopold, Dennis O'Connor (assistant majority floor leader), Frederick W. Rohlfing (minority polity leader), Jean S. King and John T. Ushijima (president).

46 Tad Szulc, "U.S. Lifts Ban on China Travel," *The New York Times*, March 16, 1971, https://www.nytimes.com/1971/03/16/archives/us-lifts-ban-on-china-travel.html.

47 *Honolulu Star-Bulletin*, September 30, 1975: "Mrs. Saiki said the trip was arranged by an organization called the American Women for International Understanding, a nonprofit organization established in 1968 in San Francisco...to form an international community of women. The group's first trip was to Moscow...she will pay her own way to and from China and expects to return home October 29."

48 Guangzhou: https://www.britannica.com/place/Guangzhou.

49 Guilin: https://www.britannica.com/place/Guilin.

50 Hangzhou: https://www.britannica.com/place/Hangzhou.

51 Xi'an: https://www.britannica.com/place/Xian-China.

52 Matt Schudel, "Virginia Knauer, top consumer adviser to three presidents, dies at 96," *The Washington Post*, https://www.washingtonpost.com/local/obituaries/virginia-knauer-top-consumer-adviser-to-three-presidents-dies-at-96/2011/10/28/gIQA1UvkTM_story.html.

53 "Helen W. Milliken, former Michigan first lady, dies at 89," *The Washington Post*, https://www.washingtonpost.com/politics/helen-w-milliken-former-michigan-firstlady-dies-at-89/2012/11/16/65bdd52a-3019-11e2-ac4a-33b8b41fb531_story.html.

54 Edith Green:https://history.house.gov/People/Detail/14080.

55 "Patsy Mink, Veteran Hawaii Congresswoman, Dies at 74," *The New York Times*, https://www.nytimes.com/2002/09/30/us/patsy-mink-veteran-hawaii-congresswoman-dies-at-74.html.

56 George H. W. Bush: https://www.newworldencyclopedia.org/entry/George_H._W._Bush.

57 Shirley Iida, "Surgeon a leader in transplants," *Honolulu Star-Bulletin*, October 28, 1999, http://archives.starbulletin.com/1999/10/28/news/story9.html.

58 "Doctor organized isles' first ambulance service," *Honolulu Star-Advertiser*, October 14, 2017, https://www.staradvertiser.com/2017/10/14/hawaii-news/doctor-organized-isles-first-ambulance-service/.

59 Shirley Iida, "Surgeon a leader in transplants," *Honolulu Star-Bulletin*, October 28, 1999, http://archives.starbulletin.com/1999/10/28/news/story9.html.

60 That is how it was reported in the *Honolulu Star-Bulletin*.

61 Ralph Ajifu, Agriculture; Richard Henderson, Economic Development; Mary George, Transportation; Ann Kobayashi, Ecology, Environment and Recreation; Buddy Soares, Public Utilities. Andy Anderson took vice chair of the Ways and Means Committee.

62 This was the Diamond Head location Governor Burns had exchanged with the Army for his dream of a medical school at the site.

63 The case originated in Alabama, where voters alleged that apportionment by county violated the equal protection clause of the Fourteenth Amendment to the U.S. Constitution because counties with lower population levels received the same representation as counties with denser populations. The court ruled 8–1 in favor of the plaintiffs, finding that legislative districts within a state must have substantially equal populations. https://ballotpedia.org/Reynolds_v._Sims

64 Chief Justice Earl Warren held that "legislators represent people, not trees or acres. Legislators are elected by voters, not farms or cities or economic interests." "Reynolds v Sims: Due Process and Legislative Apportionment," Constitutional Law Reporter, https://constitutionallawreporter.com/2016/06/21/reynolds-v-sims-due-process-legislative-apportionment-2/.

65 This was a particularly difficult race for Pat because it required defeating Senator Kenneth Brown, a Democrat, good friend and fellow Amfac board member.

66 *Honolulu Star-Bulletin* Election Report (a special-section pullout): "Mrs. Saiki topped six other candidates in the 7th District with more than 27,000 votes."

67 Erika Engle, "John Dominis shutters its doors after 31 years." *Honolulu Star-Advertiser*, December 1, 2010, https://www.staradvertiser.com/2010/12/01/business/thebuzz/john-dominis-shutters-its-doors-after-31-years/.

68 John Waihee: https://www.nga.org/governor/john-waihee/.

69 Bishop Street is described as the "nexus of Honolulu's business district." Michael Keany, "Our Town: Bishop Street," *Honolulu* Magazine, May 1, 2006, http://www.honolulumagazine.com/Honolulu-Magazine/May-2006/Our-Town-Bishop-Street/.

*Pat emerges from a voting booth during her successful race for
Hawaii's 1st Congressional District seat in the U.S. House of Representatives.*

PART III

The Congressional Years 1987–1990

A Perfect Opportunity

For nearly 30 years after Hawaii became a state in 1959, one thing was a political certainty in the Islands: An incumbent running for reelection to one of the state's two seats in the U.S. House of Representatives or the U.S. Senate had never lost an election. Never. The only way a newcomer had a prayer of winning a congressional election was if a seat became open because of death or resignation.[1]

So, on July 11, 1986,[2] when Hawaii's five-term incumbent member of the U.S. Congress, Democrat Cecil Heftel,[3] resigned his seat so he could run for governor (George Ariyoshi, who had held the position since 1974, was termed out), there was intense interest by Republicans and Democrats. Heftel's decision created a unique political situation. A special ballot to fill the remaining three months of his term in the U.S. House of Representatives would have to be added to Hawaii's primary election on Saturday, September 20. Voters in urban Honolulu's Congressional District 1 would decide who should fill the temporary seat and then—just seven weeks later—decide who should fill the two-year congressional term that would commence in January 1987. The positions could go to two different candidates.

Since statehood, Hawaii had not elected a single Republican to the U.S. House. (Republican Hiram L. Fong served in the U.S. Senate from statehood in 1959 until he retired from elective office in 1977.) My Republican friends and colleagues felt this was the perfect opportunity for me to make a move for higher office. With their encouragement came promises of financial support. My five children were grown, my husband was very supportive, and I felt it was time to spread my wings to see what I could do for Hawaii in Washington.

Dr. Franklin Kometani (who chaired my 1970 state House campaign) and Representative Andrew Poepoe offered to co-chair the campaign. I announced my intention to run on Monday, February 10, 1986, at a morning news conference held at the campaign headquarters we'd opened on Queen Emma Street in Honolulu.[4] Supporters in attendance included former U.S. senator Fong,[5] former governor William F. Quinn (Hawaii's last appointed territorial governor and the first elected after statehood),[6] incumbent state senator Ann Kobayashi and Malcolm McNaughton, former board chairman and CEO of the development company Castle & Cooke.

I recognized a tough battle would ensue. I was one of two Republicans running, and the only woman. My primary opponent was Rick Reed, then a special assistant to Honolulu prosecutor Charles Marsland.

Democrats also were gearing up for the election, and my opponents included state senator Neil Abercrombie, whom I'd unseated as chair of the senate's Higher Education Committee during the "strange coalition." Running against Abercrombie for both the special and primary elections on the Democrat ticket were Muliufi "Mufi" Hannemann, a former teacher and Harvard-educated Honolulu businessman of Samoan ancestry who had served as an aide to Governor George Ariyoshi;[7] Senator Steve Cobb, an incumbent state senator; and Louis K. "Buzzy" Agard Jr., a Hawaiian Homes commissioner and member of the Western Pacific Regional Fishery Management Council.[8] Blase Harris, a psychiatrist in private practice, ran as a nonpartisan candidate. Of the four Democrat candidates, Abercrombie was considered the front-runner, largely because of his labor union endorsements.[9]

The logistics of this Congressional District 1 race were quirky, and potentially confusing for voters, who were asked to vote twice: once for their choice to fill the temporary vacancy in Congress and again in the usual party primary to select candidates for dozens of city, state and federal offices, including that of U.S. representative.[10] To draw attention to the special congressional ballot, it was printed on pink paper. My campaign made its own effort to reduce voter confusion, launching an advertising blitz to explain the first-of-its-kind special election. We urged people to "Think Pink" and vote those ballots first.

On Wednesday, September 16, 1986, the *Honolulu Star-Bulletin* published an enthusiastic endorsement of my candidacy for both the special and the general elections. The editorial described my public service credentials but also made a case for the practical advantages of my candidacy, saying the "absence of Republicans in Hawaii's congressional delegation has been a handicap in dealing with Republican administrations." The endorsement gave my campaign a tremendous boost.

Democrat Abercrombie won the special election. Off he went to Washington, D.C., to finish the remaining weeks of Heftel's term.[11] Mufi Hannemann, however, won the bitter Democrat primary.

I won the Republican primary and moved on to campaign for the November 4 general election.

Hannemann, who was running for office for the first time, was popular and had endorsements from many of the unions. He was bright, had an engaging personality, and at six feet five inches couldn't be missed. But I saw his primary win as an advantage. It gave me an opportunity to campaign without an incumbent sitting on my back.

I was grateful to receive the unusual political endorsement of the Hawaii State Teachers Association, which traditionally supports only Democrats. I believe this exceptional endorsement was an acknowledgement of my role in building this organization with Charlie Kendall in the late 1960s and my dedication to education causes. In explaining the endorsement, union president Earl Arruda noted, "Her commitment to public school education has been demonstrated over the years by her liberal voting record on education and social issues."[12] He also praised the choice my husband and I had made to educate all five of our children in public schools, making me one of the rare state legislators who did not send their children to private schools. Hundreds of HSTA volunteers worked phone banks, held signs and served food and drinks at campaign rallies for my campaign, and for 64 other candidates the group supported in the general election.

One unique approach we took with the campaign was to host a community health fair. My physician son, Stanley Jr., and his qualified health associates organized the first of these, volunteering to check blood pressure and pulse rates, take temperatures and do other basic health screenings. It was a great hit and captured the interest of many who took advantage of this opportunity for a quick checkup. It was also a great way to attract new volunteers for the campaign. The tactic later was adopted by other candidates running for office.

It was a tough campaign, but the final results showed I had won by nearly 60 percent of the vote—a staggering success when you consider no previous Republican in our state had ever polled more than 45 percent of the vote.[13] The *Honolulu Star-Bulletin* pointed out that my election even "bucked a national trend that saw Republicans lose six seats in the (U.S.) House."[14]

Firsts, and First Steps

Off to Washington, D.C., I went. In January 1987, I was sworn in as a member of the 100th U.S. House of Representatives, representing

Hawaii's 1st Congressional District—the first Republican ever to be elected to the U.S. House from Hawaii, and only the second woman in its history as a state. I was also the first Asian American Republican woman in Congress and sat among just 23 women in a body of 435 legislators.

This made me a rather unique Republican in a Democrat-dominated state. And I guess it is what led to some remarkably special treatment by the Republican administration led by President Ronald Reagan.

I was invited to sit next to the president at the White House state dinner honoring new members of Congress. It was a unique honor and one I thoroughly enjoyed. "The president is a very stimulating dinner partner," I later told a writer for *Spirit of Aloha* magazine. "I talked to him about Hawaii, which he has visited on many occasions. He mentioned the beautiful climate, but he said he loved the people of Hawaii, the warmth of the people, as well as the place."[15] I gave President Reagan a gift—a huge koa bowl[16]—on behalf of our state and took advantage of the opportunity to emphasize Hawaii's strategic importance to the United States, and the importance of future investments in our military bases.

Upon my request, I was given membership to the Committee on Banking, Finance and Urban Affairs, and its subcommittees on Housing and Urban Development; Finance, Trade and Monetary Policy; and Economic Stabilization and Financial Institutions. One of the most significant accomplishments of this committee was passing a revised version of the well-intended, but much-maligned, Gramm-Rudman-Hollings Act of 1985, a bipartisan measure that addressed looming federal budget deficits by imposing automatic spending cuts (today called "sequester"). The original statute was ruled unconstitutional in 1986,[17] but we were able to reinstitute the Gramm-Rudman-Hollings Act of 1987 by addressing concerns about the sequestration process and the timetable for reaching a balanced budget.

In addition, I served on the Committee on Merchant Marines and Fisheries and its subcommittees on Fisheries and Wildlife Conservation, and the Environment and Oceanography. I also sat on the Special Committee on Aging. I knew each of these assignments carried significance for my constituents in Hawaii.

Two offices were assigned to me: one in the Federal Building in Honolulu and the other located in the Longworth House Office Building in Washington, D.C., One of my first tasks was staffing both of these offices. There was no shortage of candidates—nearly 700 people dropped off résumés with my Washington office during my first week on the job! I looked for loyal campaign supporters who were skilled in various capacities along with talented professionals, and was able to staff both offices with a young and capable staff. Among my senior hires were Danny Lee, a Hawaii businessman who ran my Honolulu office; Art Arnold and Dave Young, young men from the mainland who had impressive Washington experience; and Floyd Takeuchi, a *Honolulu Advertiser* reporter I pursued to help me in the area of communications.

During my time in Washington, I was particularly proud of the talented staff I was able to recruit from Hawaii. They included staff intern Keoki Kerr, who later became a well-known TV reporter with Honolulu station KITV. Caroline Lee was another local who served in the Washington, D.C., office and later headed my Honolulu staff. And I hired Bob Wernet, a former Honolulu television reporter who had served as Governor Ariyoshi's press secretary, to work in Washington during my second term.

An early priority was creating a system to handle constituent communication. Within days of being elected I started receiving calls and letters from people asking for my help. Many were requests regarding Social Security benefits, Veterans Administration benefits or military-related transfer requests.

Sometimes a development project that had been approved at the local level also required a federal stamp of approval.

And one of many responsibilities every member of the U.S. Congress holds is recommending appointments to our nation's military academies.[18] It was very important to me that this process be objective and nonpartisan. I selected a committee in Honolulu, headed by a prominent local banker, Lily Yao, to lead this effort. Based solely on the nominees' qualifications, the committee would preselect three names for each available slot and present them to me so I could make the final decision.

I knew it was an important part of my job to listen respectfully to all constituent requests and provide access to my contacts and resources whenever possible. I worked with my staff to ensure each request received a timely response. First, staff replied on my behalf to acknowledge receipt of a request. Two days later, they responded again with an update for the constituent. They would continue to communicate regularly with the constituent until the issue was resolved, one way or another. Typically, each request generated 12 to 14 pieces of mail from my office. Our autopen machine, which replicated my signature, saved the day!

Relocating to Washington, D.C., was an adjustment in itself. I was surprised to find myself something of a celebrity among journalists eager for an unusual news angle. My status as the first Japanese American Republican to represent Hawaii in the U.S. Congress garnered more attention than I expected. I was constantly asked how I'd managed to win election as a Republican in such a Democrat stronghold.

My answer? "Hard work!"

The Washington Post published a picture of me singing the "Hilo March" during an "aloha welcome" I arranged for my colleagues on the opening day of Congress.[19] With the help of Hawaiian Airlines, I had brought musicians and dancers to play Hawaiian music and dance the hula for their enjoyment in the corridor of the Longworth House Office Building. It was a great hit—it isn't every day you hear Hawaiian music and watch beautiful hula dancers performing in the halls of Congress—and quite memorable, creating camaraderie that later proved helpful. Another day, the *Post*'s influential "Style" section posted a photo of me with another Republican freshman in Congress, former *Love Boat* star Fred Grandy, who played Gopher on the popular ten-season TV series.

I couldn't figure out why everyone was so interested in me. An article in the *Spirit of Aloha* attempted to explain it: "She is … an articulate speaker and experienced legislator who's unafraid to speak her mind, [making her] a natural subject for media interest." At a time of deep partisanship, I drew attention because of my conservative approach to fiscal issues and more liberal views on social or domestic issues. The article quoted me as saying, "I think people have a difficult time categorizing me because I will take the issues one by one and I will weigh them on their merit. I see how they impact my state, and I will vote accordingly."

Adjusting to daily life in the Washington, D.C., area came with its own challenges: cold winters and the fast pace, congestion and traffic of our nation's capitol. As someone accustomed to the easy smiles and effusive, warm welcomes typical of many raised in the Islands, it took me awhile to get used to the standoffishness of many people on the streets and office buildings of Washington. A *Honolulu Star-Bulletin* article later described my reaction: "[She] persisted in letting rip with [a] cheery 'Hello!' to shocked elevator zombies, and in handing out macadamia nuts to the folks who drive the trolleys between buildings."

A highlight for me of those whirlwind days was the surprising invitation to be one of the speakers at the annual Gridiron Show, a white-tie dinner at which the nation's leading political figures, starting with the president, are the subject of good-natured ribbing. It was a star-studded event, with President Reagan in good spirits, along with most of the cabinet, some Supreme Court justices, a number of well-known journalists, the leaders in Congress, and the list went on and on.

Knowing how big a deal it was to be given a few minutes before the nation's political leadership, I sought out an experienced hand at putting together a few quips. I was pleased when I got a good laugh out of a corny joke: I was settling into the routine of Washington but still hadn't found a laundry service that knew the right amount of starch to use for my grass skirts! I know, I know, but it did get laughs. Talk about pressure!

Protecting Tuna

I had requested to be on the Merchant Marines and Fisheries Committee because Hawaii is in the middle of the Pacific, and decisions made by that committee are important to our people and our aquatic and fishing industries.

The committee influences decisions made by all of the existing U.S. Fishery Management Council regions around our nation: New England, Mid-Atlantic, South Atlantic, Gulf of Mexico, Caribbean, Pacific and North Pacific.[20] The councils were created by the Magnuson-Stevens Fishery Conservation and Management Act, first passed in 1976 to assure local participation in matters governing fishing in U.S. federal waters, specifically maintaining populations of fish and sustainability of fishing industries.

Every fish on the planet was at that time included under the Magnuson Act, with the exception of tuna (*ahi* in Hawaiian)—a fish vital to our people. Ahi is a favorite among locals and is used in sashimi (thinly sliced raw fish served without rice), which is especially coveted during the New Year holidays. Worry persisted that without protection against rampant harvesting of tuna, the species could become seriously diminished.

I learned that a U.S. fishing industry lobby representing the Gulf of Mexico area had inordinate influence in Washington. This powerful and politically connected lobby was responsible for the exclusion of tuna from the Magnuson Act. There was no other good reason to exclude the species from the act other than to enrich Gulf tuna interests, which had virtual control over the market.

Hawaii's senior senator, Daniel Inouye, contacted me to explain the thorny issue and make me even more aware of how much this affected Hawaii. He apprised me of past efforts to amend the Magnuson Act to include tuna. These efforts had all failed to pass out of the House of Representatives.

Forces in Hawaii were led by the United Fishing Agency headed by Frank Goto, whose efforts over time had helped take commercial fishing from locally based wooden sampans to a national fleet of ocean going longline fishing vessels, making Hawaiian seafood an internationally recognized delicacy.[21] Goto, along with agency assistant manager Brooks Takenaka[22] and Kitty Simonds, chairman of the Western Pacific Regional Fishery Management Council responsible for monitoring the habits and status of all fish in Hawaiian waters,[23] expressed to me their concern about the tuna situation.

Walter B. Jones Sr. of North Carolina, chairman of the House Merchant Marines Committee,[24] was a sympathetic Democrat but he could not get a majority of his Democrat colleagues to support the move to include tuna in the Magnuson Act. So, we decided to combine forces. We put together the favorable Democrat votes and my favorable Republican votes and passed the bill out of committee.

Chairman Jones suggested I seek a hearing before the House Rules Committee to advance the measure on the consent calendar. That way it could be approved by unanimous consent, which allows a bill to pass without a formal vote. I gained the crucial support of the Rules Committee.

When the Gulf area tuna lobby learned of my moves, they made an immediate effort to confront me. They came to my office in force—in their Gucci shoes, Gucci jackets and Gucci briefcases—and insisted on an audience. When I couldn't see them immediately because of other scheduled appointments, they seemed disappointed, but were not insistent. After all, they no doubt thought, what damage could a freshman legislator from a distant island in the Pacific do to overturn their long-held control over the industry?

On the day of the vote, I posted supportive members of the Merchant Marines Committee at the entrance doors to the House Chamber, armed with leaflets explaining that for environmental reasons—the continued existence of this vital fish, the tuna—it was necessary for them to vote "aye" by unanimous consent on this measure.

It worked. The bill passed by unanimous consent and I called Senator Inouye to tell him the good news: Tuna was finally included for protection by the Magnuson Act. I told him to anticipate a call from the tuna lobby. He was ready.

The fishing industries in the islands were thrilled with the outcome and ordinary families in Hawaii were assured plenty of ahi sashimi during the New Year holidays. In fact, each New Year holiday I'm reminded of our efforts to protect our tuna resources. The leadership of the United Fishing Agency still sends me a generous serving of sashimi made from tuna caught in the Pacific.[25]

Nicaragua

In January 1985, two years before I was sworn in as a member of the House of Representatives, President Reagan had given a stirring State of the Union address that set the tone for U.S. foreign policy, establishing what came to be known as the Reagan Doctrine. Key to that policy was support for "freedom fighters" around the globe.[25]

"Freedom is not the sole prerogative of a chosen few; it is the universal right of all God's children," he said. America's mission was to "nourish and defend freedom and democracy ... stand by all our democratic allies ... and ... not break faith with those who are risking their lives—on every continent, from Afghanistan to Nicaragua—to defy Soviet-supported aggression and secure rights which have been ours from birth." He urged the nation to think of support for freedom fighters as self-defense and implored Congress "to support the democratic forces whose struggle is tied to our own security."

The pronouncement laid a foundation for a program of military assistance around the world—from Afghan rebels in their fight against Soviet occupiers, to anti-Communist Angolan forces embroiled in that nation's civil war, to covert support for Nicaragua's Contra rebels, who were attempting to overthrow the leftist Sandinista regime and the iron fist of its president, Daniel Ortega, who had shut down communications and imposed a socialistic form of government on its people.

Ortega alleged U.S. involvement would lead to the ruination of his country's economy. Domestic critics claimed supporting freedom fighters prolonged and escalated bloody conflicts and put the U.S. on the side of repressive, undemocratic elements.[26] Nevertheless, under the leadership of U.S. Marine Corps Lt. Col. Oliver North, President Reagan and the United States continued to aid the rebels.

On June 26, 1986, while I was in Hawaii campaigning for Congress, the U.S. House of Representatives approved a new aid package to Nicaragua's Contra rebels: $70 million in military aid and $30 million in nonlethal assistance to the Contras. In Nicaragua, the response was quick and decisive: The Sandinista government shut down *La Prensa*, Nicaragua's only opposition newspaper, and announced stricter internal security measures to fight what he described as "a new aggressive escalation."[27]

Later, as a congresswoman, I was busy attending to committee assignments when I received a personal call from President Reagan, who asked that I join a select group of fellow Republican members of Congress to make a trip to Nicaragua to meet with the Contra rebel leaders.

We swooped in by military plane to the humid Nicaraguan jungle, where Contra headquarters were organized in tents. Though we were outfitted with bulletproof vests and escorted by armed guards, we were not fully prepared to navigate this wild jungle and deal with its mud, rain and pests. Many of us were dressed in business suits; the women had to negotiate the terrain in high-heeled shoes! One member of Congress could not deal with it and had to be carried to the tents for the meetings. Perhaps because of my early adventures in the sugarcane fields, I proved less flappable than many of my colleagues and felt quite prepared to meet the challenges of the rugged landscape.

As we sat with Contra leaders and posed our questions, we could feel the tension and the zeal with which these young freedom fighters were committed to their cause. They explained their need for assistance from the United States to overthrow the existing regime. The meeting was brief, but informative, and it certainly got the attention of our group. We returned convinced that President Reagan's commitment to the Contra forces against the Sandinistas was worthy of our support.

At home, however, support for the Nicaraguan Contras was criticized for being futile and expensive. It led to much dialogue as to whether the United States should impose its form of government on other countries. The debate continues today.

The Kingdom of Tonga

In the spring of 1988, President Reagan asked me to make another trip—this time to personally represent him in the Kingdom of Tonga in the South Pacific, where King Taufaʻahau Tupou IV [28] would soon be celebrating his 70th birthday.

I was entrusted to accomplish three goals. First, to mark the centenary of the friendship treaty (the Treaty of Amity, Commerce and Navigation) between the United States and the Kingdom of Tonga.

Second, to present a resolution adopted by the U.S. House of Representatives that noted the long and friendly ties with the kingdom and offered America's best wishes on the king's 70th birthday. The Resolution also recognized the 21st anniversary of the king's coronation and extended the best wishes of the Congress to the king and the people of Tonga.

Third, and most importantly, I was entrusted to represent the United States and President Reagan during the weeklong celebration of the king's 70th birthday on July 4, 1988.

I was, of course, honored and excited to represent our country and our president on this important mission. It is likely I received this honor because I represented Hawaii, which has many Tongan immigrants. But I also had a booster in the National Security Council. James Kelly, a Naval Academy graduate who had made Hawaii his home after his naval service, was the NSC's point man on Asia-Pacific issues. Jim went to bat for me, I later learned, with the president and State Department.[29]

As delegation leader I could bring a staffer to accompany me and assist me in my official duties. Fortunately, my executive assistant, Floyd K. Takeuchi, was available. Before he joined my congressional staff, he was a respected journalist with the *Honolulu Advertiser*. He also had many years of experience as a journalist in the Pacific Islands and had traveled to Tonga. He was most important to me, but especially on this trip. His knowledge of cultural protocol helped me avoid any serious unintentional social errors.

My presidential delegation included Maureen Zatarga, associate director in the White House Office of Personnel, and my friend and the former governor of American Samoa, Peter Tali Coleman, who joined us in Fiji. Leonard Rochwarger, U.S. ambassador to both Fiji and Tonga, joined us in Tonga.

Getting from Washington, D.C., to Nuku'alofa, the capital of Tonga, was no easy matter, as we soon learned. We flew by commercial airlines from Dulles International Airport to Los Angeles, and then on to Honolulu. We immediately changed planes and continued on another commercial flight to Nadi, Fiji. There, we were able to rest for a few hours at the beautiful Regent of Fiji Resort.[30] We were then greeted by an executive Lear jet sent by the U.S. Air Force and piloted by two young officers from Yokota Air Force Base in Japan. They were sent to fly our delegation from Fiji to Tonga, the final leg of our long journey.

As we approached Tongatapu, the main island in the kingdom, the pilots asked if we'd like a tour. Of course I agreed, and soon we were flying very low over the island, showing off the "United States of America" lettering on the side of the plane. We were easily and eagerly recognized by the people, who waved and saluted us. I think it was unmistakable that AMERICA had arrived to salute their king.

We landed at Fua'amotu International Airport on a bright, clear day and were met by Crown Prince Siaosi[31] and his entourage. The crown prince was a tall, dashing gentleman—a royal who graduated from Britain's Royal Military Academy Sandhurst.

We were taken to the royal lounge, where we were treated to refreshments while staff unloaded our luggage from the Air Force jet. Interestingly, we saw a U.S. Marine Corps C-130 transport on the tarmac and ran into Lt. Col. Rick Stepien, USMC, a senior public affairs officer assigned to the Pacific Command at Camp Smith in Hawaii.

Col. Stepien had accompanied the Fleet Marine Forces Pacific Band, which flew to Tonga to participate in the festivities that week.

After refreshments in the VIP lounge and engaging conversations with the crown prince, we were escorted outside to board waiting cars forming a motorcade to the International Dateline Hotel in Nuku'alofa.[32]

This is where Floyd helped me avoid my first *faux pas*. In my own personal and informal style, I hailed my good friend Governor Coleman, inviting him to sit in my car with me. Floyd gently informed me that as leader I represented the president of the United States and had the Mercedes to myself while the rest of the delegation was assigned to Hyundai sedans. The motorcade proceeded, led by a police officer on a motorcycle with sirens blaring, all the way to the hotel. I learned the lesson and respected my role, leading every motorcade thereafter. That's how we got around the entire time we were in the kingdom.

The following events were a blur of Polynesian pageantry, starting with the formal meeting with the king at the palace. We were officially presented to the court and had the opportunity to express President Reagan's birthday wishes. We presented the resolution from Congress along with a huge American eagle sculpture in bisque porcelain as a gift from the president and the people of the United States to the king and the people of Tonga. As an aside, I must credit our protocol officer, Clark Wurzberger of the State Department, who hand carried the huge eagle on various plane rides and had it occupy a seat next to his from Washington, D.C., It was too large and too precious to crate and put in the back of our various planes as baggage.

One of the highlights for me of that remarkable week in Tonga included attending a Free Wesleyan Church service in honor of the king. Here again, Floyd came to the rescue, for in order to be properly dressed, I needed a hat to enter this beautiful church. He used his initiative and solicited one from the wife of one of our military aides, U.S. Air Force Col. Thomas "Tom" Wood.[33] With the borrowed hat, which somehow, miraculously, coordinated perfectly with my dress, I made my entrance properly attired.

A royal ball was on the agenda at the International Dateline Hotel, where the Tongan Defense Forces Band and the Fleet Marine Force Pacific Band from Hawaii had a friendly battle of the bands. This was followed by two consecutive days of royal feasts at midday for more than 1,000 guests on the grounds of the Royal Palace. Women from around the kingdom served each delegation. The feasts marked the first—and, in fact, the only—time in my life that I've seen guests come to an event in their finest attire, be seated on beautiful tapa mats and be presented with *individual* roasted suckling pigs!

During the feasts the king invited me to join him on the royal dais—a significant gesture, as it turned out, because I was the only head of a foreign delegation to be so honored. I have to assume that the king wanted to recognize the importance of his nation's relations with the United States of America.

Another event that impressed me was a naval review of ships in Nuku'alofa harbor. Tonga has a small naval force, but the review was intended to salute His Majesty by showcasing foreign warships representing nations in the Asia-Pacific region—including Australia, New Zealand, France and Britain—and a U.S. Navy warship, the USS *Brewton*, an impressive frigate out of Pearl Harbor. I was particularly proud of Commander Paul D. Mallett, the *Brewton*'s skipper, and the officers and sailors of FF1086 when the royal launch passed the American warship with its crew along the railings, all wearing bright white uniforms, smartly saluting His Majesty. Among all the delegation leaders, only I was invited to be aboard the royal launch with the king.

I learned the full significance of all the recognition the king had given me as the representative of President Reagan and our country when one evening at a diplomatic event the head of another delegation greeted me with a telling comment: "Congresswoman Saiki, so good to finally meet you. We've only seen you from afar."

Our magical week finally came to an end. As we flew back to

Washington, D.C., Floyd and I recalled the many events and experiences we had enjoyed. It was time to "come back to earth." There would be no more limousines waiting or motorcades with sirens and officers clearing the way. It was time to walk to my car in the congressional parking lot at Dulles and drive myself home.

Reparations, After 40 Years

Since that terrible day when my uncle Narikawa and his family were hauled off to an internment camp in Utah, I had sworn that I would find a way to correct the historic inequities our government perpetrated on American citizens of Japanese ancestry during World War II. From the moment I was elected to Congress, I knew I had a platform to do just that. I was determined to champion proposed reparations legislation, which had been discussed over many years, but always failed to pass.

The excuse I heard was lack of support from Republican members of the U.S. House of Representatives. To me, that meant either a lack of understanding or a refusal to accept responsibility for a serious violation of constitutional rights guaranteed to our citizens. The unjustifiable internment of citizens of our country denied Japanese Americans their rights under the law, subjecting them to confiscation of their property and investments. Many were denied due process and were transported to so-called camps to be held, many under miserable conditions.

This injustice was inflicted on tens of thousands of families, whose unjustified incarceration was indefinite. All this because their country of ancestral origin had attacked Pearl Harbor. The whole thing smelled of bipartisan racism.

I asked Representative Robert H. "Bob" Michel,[34] who was our Republican leader, to allow me to speak to our congressional caucus on this subject. He graciously agreed. I faced my new colleagues and asked them to fasten their seat belts because I intended to take them on a wild emotional ride that might leave them with feelings of guilt.

I took the opportunity to remind my fellow Republicans of the determination, bravery and sacrifice made by AJA (Americans of Japanese Ancestry) men who volunteered as members of the much recognized and honored U.S. Army's 100th Battalion and the 442nd Regimental Combat Team. (Hawaii's two U.S. senators at that time, Dan Inouye and Spark Matsunaga, were both decorated veterans of those units.) These were true Americans who saw their families being mistreated by our government but nevertheless were willing to sacrifice their lives for their country. Their commitment and loyalty were proven beyond doubt and with blood.

I gave firsthand testimony about more than 110,000 citizens of Japanese ancestry—mostly from the West Coast and Hawaii, including my uncle and his family—who were sent to internment camps. Some called them "horse stables." I called them concentration camps. My colleagues listened intently to the details of this travesty, finally gaining a more vivid picture of what had transpired.

My plea for justice affected enough Republicans to change their votes, and we passed the Civil Liberties Protection Act of 1988.[35] The act focused on an official apology to Japanese American families who suffered injustices and provided for token reparations of $20,000 per interned person, including children.

After the measure passed, I received a call from White House staff urging me to call President Reagan to request that he sign the legislation rather than letting it become law without his signature. I placed the call and the president agreed to sign the bill. A photograph showing him signing the bill can be found prominently displayed at the Smithsonian and every AJA museum in the country—and in Japan.

The president requested that I stand next to him as he signed the bill. It was a great day for me to have achieved a personal commitment to right this wrong.

Reelection to Congress

My first two years in Congress swept by at a rapid pace and before I knew it, it was time for reelection campaigning. Throughout my first term I had always maintained efforts to stay in touch with the local people and press, and religiously flew home about every three weeks (during regular recesses) to hold meetings in Honolulu. All of this would help as I began preparations for another round of fundraising and constituent group meetings.

As I earlier noted, since 1959, when Hawaii achieved statehood, incumbents had sought reelection to Congress 31 times. None had ever lost. But it is widely known in political circles that an incumbent is most vulnerable after his or her first election, and I had no doubt a Democrat opponent would try to unseat me and return the delegation to the Democrat Party. The battle was on.

By August of 1988, there were three Democrats ready to challenge me for the seat: Mary Bitterman, former head of Voice of America and director of the Hawaii State Department of Commerce and Consumer Affairs; John Radcliffe, a labor leader and former head of the Hawaii State Teachers Association; and Leigh-Wai Doo, a lawyer and city councilman. One Libertarian candidate, Blase Harris, also filed to run against me.

The *Honolulu Advertiser*–Channel 2 Hawaii Poll that month indicated my campaign was "running well ahead of anybody the Democrats can nominate to face her," but I never took anything for granted. Mary Bitterman had the endorsement of Governor John Waihee and Senator Daniel Inouye, who took an active role in her campaign. He even did something very unusual during one of his returns to Hawaii: He stood beside the highway with a sign supporting Bitterman. It raised many eyebrows, for it was quite unusual to have one of such prestige—and only one arm, the other lost as he served with distinction in the U.S. Army in World War II [36]—standing at the curbside waving at motorists driving home from work.

It was a good try and expressed his deep commitment to support his candidate, defeat the Republican and return to an all-Democrat congressional team from Hawaii.

The race took a lot of organization and fundraising. I had to reach 220,000 voters, and the best way to do that was through expenditures in mass media advertising and direct mail.[37] Harvey Hukari, the political consultant who helped me in the first race in 1986, was again helpful in presenting a positive image.

The brochures he developed to tell my story always included references to the values of hard work, sacrifice, education, honor and respect I learned from my parents. Fundraising is always a challenge, but many individuals and business types contributed generously, and I was able to raise the most funds of all candidates in the race.

Bitterman got endorsements from the Democrat establishment, including the huge and influential International Longshore and Warehouse Union, which also gave her financial support. The others, John Radcliffe and Leigh-Wai Doo, received support from liberal and union political action committees out of Washington.

Bitterman handily won the primary over her two other opponents and the general election became a three-person race among her, me and Blase Harris, the Libertarian candidate.

In my opinion, what turned the race in my favor occurred when my opponent overreacted to a brochure my campaign had printed, but not distributed, to voters. It was entitled "The Mary Bitterman Record."[38] My consultant had more than 60,000 copies printed on the mainland and sent in bags to my campaign office for mailing.

I reviewed the brochure before giving the OK for its mailing. Its charges of Bitterman's failure to comply with the legislative auditor's recommendations, her failure to safeguard the state's financial institutions for which she was charged, and other failures during her tenure as director of Commerce and Consumer Affairs were accurate, but I felt the brochure was too negative in tone, and directed that it not be distributed.

My attitude was to keep campaigning as positively as possible and not use my funds for crippling negative attacks on my opponents. But somehow, Bitterman got hold of the brochure and called a press conference at which she presented it to a befuddled press. They had not seen or heard of the brochure the candidate presented to them as evidence of negative attacks.

The event backfired spectacularly when it became obvious the brochures had never been distributed. Bitterman broke down in tears and left the news conference. When the press came to me, asking for an explanation, I admitted the brochures had been printed and more than 80 bags of them were at my headquarters, if anyone wished to examine them. "I just wanted to win, not kill anyone's reputation in the process," I told reporters.

The press had a field day with my opponent's political blunder. The quote of the day came from Joe Moore of KHON-TV, when on his 6 p.m. newscast he held up the never-mailed brochure and declared it was "the first time that a candidate smeared herself." I, too, learned an important lesson: Always check out the facts before taking a public stand.

I got an unexpected publicity boost when I was asked to be secretary of the Republican National Convention in New Orleans that August. It could only help my reputation and name recognition to be the person who called the roll for each state on national television. This was also the month I learned I would be with President Reagan as he signed the Japanese reparations bill, an honor the *Star-Bulletin* described as "fitting and another political plus."

Still, the campaign remained vigorous and difficult. It was me against "the machine" and Democrats never failed to support their candidates because they felt so strongly that an all-Democrat contingent in Congress was best for Hawaii. My greatest disappointment was the endorsement of my opponent by two organizations for whom I had exerted strong support and assistance during my legislative years: the HGEA (government workers) and the Hawaii State Teachers Association. I knew that leadership of both organizations were committed to the Democrats, but hoped their members remained available to me because they knew of my various efforts on their behalf.

My supporters, however, were loyal and generous. I had the confidence of the Republican Party, but also maintained support from a cross-section of the voting community who voted for the "person" rather than the "party." I even garnered support from progressive organizations including Earthtrust, a Honolulu-based international wildlife-protection group, which appreciated my push to lower dolphin kills in the Marine Mammal Protection Act, and the national Sierra Club, which had awarded me a Clean Air Champion medal for efforts to bring clean-air legislation to the House floor.

I was elected to a second term and again went through the ceremonial aspects of getting sworn in. I requested the same committees I'd held before so I could continue my efforts in finance, merchant marine concerns, aging and education.

Emperor Hirohito's State Funeral

In February of 1989, shortly after starting my second term as a member of the Republican minority in the House of Representatives, I had the distinct pleasure and honor of being named by Minority Leader Bob Michel to represent U.S. House Republicans at the state funeral of Japanese Emperor Hirohito. Most likely the honor came because of my status as the only Japanese American in the Republican caucus, and because I grew up in Hawaii, where Japanese culture is recognized and respected. Nevertheless, I felt overwhelmed by the privilege, given that I did not hold a leadership position in the caucus. The decision was Leader Michel's and had the approval of my colleagues in the House.

I was invited to join President George H. W. Bush and First Lady Barbara Bush and other colleagues on Air Force One as part of the official delegation to Tokyo. It was my first trip on Air Force One and, I must say, I was impressed during a tour of the Boeing 707 aircraft. It had all the amenities, including an office, a conference room, a private bedroom with bath and a full galley where food was prepared for passengers. Desks lined the side of the front section, where informal meetings could take place, and in the rear of the plane was a vast area for the press.

It was a gloomy, rainy day when we landed at Yokota Air Force Base outside of Tokyo and after a short visit to the duty-free shop we

were introduced to the latest technical and innovative electronic gad-
gets not yet available on the open market. At that time the Japanese
were way ahead of everyone in the development of radio and audio
equipment. Some of my colleagues had a field day purchasing some of
the interesting, innovative items. One of the delegates had forgotten
his credit card and requested my help. Of course, I obliged, and he
did pay me back.

Before the funeral ceremonies, I was invited to meet with members
of the Japanese Diet.[39] I accepted, not only for the honor but for the
curiosity of where they would seat me, as a woman legislator, in the
formal setting of a meeting.

We would be seated on the floor, at a long table. Being of Japanese
ancestry and informed by my traditional grandparents, I knew that
women always sat on the lower (ocean) side of a table. Men always sat
on the mountain side. That was the custom—just as it was the custom
for women to walk three steps behind their husbands.

The problem was solved by their decision to seat me at the *side*
of the table—thus avoiding the custom and its accompanying per-
ceptions of gender discrimination. I thought it was a most sensitive
gesture.

Emperor Hirohito had died of cancer in January, at age 87, following a reign of 62 years, including a period before and after World
War II when he was despised by much of the rest of the world as a
symbol of Japanese military aggression.[40] But the emperor was loved
and respected in his home country, as demonstrated by more than
200,000 people who lined the streets in the center of Tokyo that
Friday, February 24, as the imperial hearse and its motorcade traveled from the Imperial Palace to Shinjuku Gyoen park.[41] Two funeral
services—one religious and one secular—were held before about
10,000 invited guests and foreign dignitaries representing more than
163 nations.

President and Mrs. Bush received special recognition, and we in
the U.S. delegation were accorded with respect. The weather was
harsh—dark, rainy, gloomy and exceedingly cold. We huddled under

large tents and were provided with extra blankets, hand warmers and heaters. The ceremonies, conducted in Japanese, were difficult to follow but the somber pageantry was impressive. The entire experience was unprecedented and will always be treasured.

Johnston Atoll

Later in my second term in Congress, I responded to the concerns of my constituents regarding Johnston Island, an atoll of 1,300 acres made up of four islands about 750 miles southwest of the Hawaiian Islands.

The atoll was once used for nuclear and biological testing. In the 1970s, the focus changed, and the island was used for storing and burning chemical weapons. Nuclear weapons, Agent Orange defoliants and containers of mustard gas were all part of this weapons destruction program.

A new, $150 million incinerator was due to open in early May of 1990. The possibility of toxic material being carried through incineration into the atmosphere, and reaching our Islands, was a major concern. The Army had plans to ship additional stockpiles of chemical weapons for destruction, including the nerve agent sarin—which causes death by paralyzing the respiratory system—from Europe.[42]

I requested a formal congressional fact-finding visit to Johnston Island. The trip was called the "Saiki Codel" for "Saiki Congressional Delegation." The five of us on the trip were given a thorough briefing, site visitation and assurances that maximum care was taken to avoid any release of burnt material into the air.

After examining the incinerators and procedures, I was satisfied I could allay the concerns of my constituents. What convinced me was the fact that all the personnel who lived and worked on Johnston Atoll seemed perfectly content with the safety precautions. They frequently played golf on their little open-air, three-hole golf course.

I returned to Washington, D.C., and issued a report to our local citizens describing the detailed findings of my trip. I felt I had done my constituents an important service and answered their call for help.

Choosing a New Challenge

My second term as a member of the U.S. House of Representatives was coming to a close and I was looking forward to seeking another term when Senator Spark Matsunaga unexpectedly passed away. We knew he was not well—he'd been diagnosed in early 1990 with prostate cancer—but we fully expected him to recover. Instead, his condition deteriorated rapidly and on April 3 of that year, he cast his final Senate vote from a wheelchair, unable to speak. He died just 12 days later.[43, 44]

Sparky was well loved by his constituents and had the reputation of being a gracious host to all Hawaii visitors to Washington, D.C., Most people didn't know this, but he and I were good friends. Sparky had gone to school with my husband on Kauai. And during my time in Congress, Sparky always offered support and friendship.

His passing raised many questions about who would complete the four years left in his term in the Senate. Governor John Waihee moved quickly to appoint Daniel Akaka, my colleague in the House, to take his place, so there would be an incumbent Democratic senator in place.

The race for Matsunaga's seat would take place in just five months. Words of encouragement came pouring in from my Republican colleagues, who urged me to run for the seat. Even my friends in the U.S. Senate—led by Robert Dole and Phil Gramm—offered financial support if I were to consider the race. The campaign would require substantial commitments, not only in time and energy, but in dollars. With the short time available, the effort seemed impossible to accomplish.

Seeking reelection to my House seat would have been the easy way to go. Retaining the hard-fought seat would not be as difficult this time around.

However, the temptation of accomplishing more as a U.S. senator gnawed at me as a tempting challenge. A vote carries more leverage among 100 others in the Senate than it does among 435 votes in the House.

Again, it was my husband Stanley who brought things into perspective.

He reminded me that my purpose in getting elected in the first place was not to seek power or personal recognition but to find answers to the problems facing our people. "If you win, that's great," he said, "but if you lose, what have you really lost? You're doing this for the good of our people—not for yourself."

The most compelling encouragement came from the Oval Office itself, when President George H. W. Bush requested that I come by for a chat. He had asked John H. Sununu, former governor of New Hampshire[44] and now his chief of staff (and a friend of mine), to sit in on the meeting when he asked me to consider running for Senator Matsunaga's seat in the Senate. I told him how difficult it would be for a Republican to win in such a blue state as Hawaii. Only one Republican, Hiram L. Fong, had ever been elected to the U.S. Senate from Hawaii. The difficulty would be aggravated by a short campaign cycle.

President Bush was well aware of the challenges that faced me and offered all the help he could muster. He asked me what he could do to help me get elected. I didn't hesitate to tell him what he could do to help the people of Hawaii.

Reclaiming Kahoolawe

I told President Bush about Kahoolawe, a 45-square-mile island southwest of Maui. The U.S. military took over Kahoolawe shortly after the bombing of Pearl Harbor and the declaration of martial law. In 1953, President Dwight D. Eisenhower issued an executive order transferring the island to the U.S. Navy,[45] which used the area for target practice, especially during biennial Rim of the Pacific (RIMPAC) training exercises.[46] Kahoolawe became known as the Target Island, subject to the assault of air-dropped bombs, TNT charges, underwater torpedoes and other weapons.

I asked for an immediate end to the bombing, which was a painful violation of the cultural sensibilities of the Hawaiian people, who

wanted to restore the natural state of the island and preserve its thousands of historical and cultural artifacts.[47] The continued bombing of
Kahoolawe was one of the most sensitive political issues of that era
in Hawaii. Most residents felt the need to use the island for military
target practice had long since been met.

I knew from close consultations with community leaders such
as Maui mayor Hannibal Tavares and noted Hawaiian sovereignty
advocate and attorney Mililani Trask that public support to end the
bombing was broad and deep. If a presidential order had started
all of this, I reasoned, President Bush could stop it the same way.
My request meant the bombing exercises, created as a multinational
effort to ensure the safety of sea lanes, would have to be conducted
elsewhere.

The whole concern came as quite a surprise to President Bush, who
was not aware of the bombings and the protracted disturbance to our
people. I pointed out the even greater concern over fears of an errant
bomb landing in the midst of nearby (and well-populated) Maui. The
bombing exercises were already rattling residential windows and doors
along the Maui coast. Maui residents could feel the earth shaking
and see flashes of light when the bombs hit Kahoolawe. Furthermore,
Maui is home to the Kaanapali Golf Course. The president was an
avid golfer, so this caught his attention.

He immediately turned to his chief of staff and asked him to look
into the matter. Sununu first asked me to spell Kahoolawe, which I
did. He assured me it would receive his immediate attention.

Curiously, the Democrat delegation to Congress never had pursued
the president to revoke the executive order. I have to wonder: Did they
not do their homework? Or did they simply choose not to pursue this
important issue while under Republican leadership for fear of giving
credit to the opposition party?

I made the request in May of 1990. Within four months, on September 22, 1990, President Bush issued a directive to Richard Cheney,
then secretary of defense, to stop the bombing of the island. The president was quoted in the *Honolulu Star-Bulletin*: "You are directed to

discontinue the use of Kahoolawe as a weapons range effective immediately. This directive extends to the use of the island for small arms,
artillery, naval gunfire."

Bush went on to say he would "require Defense Secretary Cheney
to create a joint Department of Defense–State of Hawaii commission
to examine the future status of Kahoolawe and related issues."

It pleased me to accomplish in four months what my Democrat
colleagues had been attempting for years. I was grateful to President
Bush for taking immediate action. Upon my request he also agreed to
make a personal visit to Honolulu. His endorsement at a fundraiser
on my behalf would be most helpful. A race of this nature required
millions of dollars.

I made another policy proposal I felt would be helpful to establish
the United States firmly in the Pacific region. I suggested that President Bush take the opportunity to meet with leaders of the mostly
recently independent Pacific island nations. No effort had been made
thus far by any U.S. president to gather together Pacific island leaders
to coordinate diplomacy, or even listen to their concerns regarding
the Pacific region and its future. I recommended the engagement of
the East-West Center, next to the University of Hawaii at Manoa
campus, for input as to who should be invited and when and where
to have this gathering.

My suggestion was received wholeheartedly and the event took
place in October 1990 at the East-West Center with the participation
of 11 Pacific island leaders representing Papua New Guinea, Palau,
Guam, Tonga, the Federated States of Micronesia, Fiji, Republic of
the Marshall Islands, Vanuatu, Nauru, Niue, the Solomon Islands,
Tuvalu, Samoa and the Cook Islands. Dr. Victor Li, president of the
East-West Center, spearheaded the conference. I also worked with senior researcher Dr. Charles Morrison, who later was named president.
The Center had a program focused on Oceania, but it had never involved the president of the United States.[48]

This initial regional gathering called by President Bush led to the
future, more permanent organization called the United States/Paci-

fic Island Nations Joint Commercial Commission (US/PIN JCC), which is now recognized as an entity to consult whenever economic or military concerns arise in the Pacific. It is unique in that it was the first multilateral joint commercial commission to promote mutually beneficial commercial and economic relations between the United States and the Pacific Island nations.[49] The US/PIN JCC came about because our president had the imagination and the willingness to lead the United States into active involvement in the Pacific region.

During the same visit, the president graciously appeared as the principal attraction at a $125-per-head fundraiser to help meet the cost of my Senate campaign, which was anticipated to exceed $5 million. The dinner was held at the Hilton Hawaiian Village Coral Ballroom in Waikiki and attended by more than 1,200 people, with Dr. Franklin Kometani, a longtime supporter and my campaign chairman, serving as master of ceremonies.

It proved to be a most interesting fundraiser, with no candidate present! I was in touch with the event by phone—calling in from Washington, D.C., where Congress was in the midst of a roll call vote on the deficit-reduction budget bill. There was no way I could fly home in time, so the phone call had to suffice.

It happened to be a crucial budget vote—one that forced a tax increase, which the president had promised to avoid. He made the statement "Read my lips—no new taxes" as a campaign promise. But, as happens in politics, he had to go back on his word and support the final budget to keep our nation afloat. It was a difficult decision for him and may have cost him a second term. It tore at me to vote against the president's recommendation, but it was the right thing to do under the circumstances.

It was a turning point in my campaign, as well as the president's reelection bid. My husband and I hurriedly returned to Honolulu. I did my best to conduct a vigorous, very personal campaign and I believe I made an effective effort.

The campaign itself looked very promising, with early polls showing I was leading Senator Daniel Akaka, who had represented the 2nd

Congressional District in Hawaii (rural Oahu and Neighbor Islands) in the House for 14 years before his appointment to the Senate that May. I was ahead with women and Japanese American voters, traditionally the backbone of Democratic campaigns in the Islands. Money was available and endorsements from business and educational groups were showing strength. The predictions were that I could win this close battle.

Much as I was eager and ready to engage Akaka in policy issues for better public understanding of the issues—including our differing opinions on the best way to address the national deficit—he refused to appear with me in public debate. All media efforts made in this direction were frustrated by the Akaka campaign. This race once again exposed, as so often happens in politics in Hawaii, the basic strength of the union organizations with the iron grip of the Democrat party machine in action.

I lost the election by nine percentage points. It was a difficult loss, but not the end of political life for me. 🌿

Pat in early 1990 led a congressional delegation to Johnston Atoll southwest of Hawaii, where the U.S. was to burn a huge stockpile of chemical weapons.

Pat, the wife of a physician and mother to two medical doctors, was the first elected official in Hawaii to offer voters a chance to check their blood pressure as part of a political campaign. Here, during her campaign for the U.S. Senate in 1990, Pat's blood pressure is checked by her son, Dr. Stanley Saiki Jr.

Pat poses with Uncle Sam while sign waving on South King Street in Honolulu during her successful 1986 race for the U.S. House of Representatives.

Supporters line up for sign waving on a rainy day in Hilo during Pat's campaign for the U.S. Senate in 1990.

First Lady Barbara Bush, a close friend of Pat's, often campaigned for Pat in Hawaii. Here, during the 1990 race for the U.S. Senate, Pat and campaign chairman Dr. Franklin Kometani introduce Mrs. Bush during an event.

Pat arrives at Hickam Air Force Base in Hawaii aboard Air Force One
with President George H. W. Bush and First Lady Barbara Bush. They were
on their way to Japan for the state funeral of Emperor Hirohito.

President Ronald Reagan invited Pat to stand next to him as he signed legislation approving an official apology and reparations for the internment of Japanese Americans during World War II. The president was going to let the bill become law without his signature but Pat asked him to hold a signing ceremony at the White House. Among the members of Congress attending the signing in 1988 were Hawaii senator Sparky Matsunaga, far left, Representative Norman Mineta of California (between Matsunaga and Pat), and at far right, California representative Robert Matsui.

Pat Saiki
United States Senate

Send Hawaii's Best

Paid for by the National Republican Senatorial Committee

NRSC
425 2nd Street, N.E.
Washington, D.C. 20002

Non-Profit Org.
U.S. Postage
PAID
Honolulu, HI
Permit #2232

Pat Saiki's parents, Shizue and Kazuo Fukuda, on their wedding day.

HONOR AND RESPECT

I owe a great deal to my mother and father.

When I was a kid in Hilo, Japanese families put a lot more emphasis on the advancement of their sons.

My parents were different. They had three daughters.

My father was determined to break the cultural stereotypes and make certain that my sisters and I became educated and independent.

Through my family's hard work and sacrifice, we succeeded.

The three of us graduated from college. We all became school teachers.

Through my years in public life and community service, I never forgot the importance of what my parents gave me and the values that they passed on to their daughters.

Pride, education, hard work, honor and respect.

They are the same values that I've tried to pass on to my five children.

And they are the same values that will guide me as your new Senator in our nation's capital.

On November 6, you can elect me as the first woman from Hawaii to sit in the United States Senate. I am honored to have the opportunity to serve.

Please give me your trust and support.

Thank you,

Pat Saiki

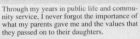

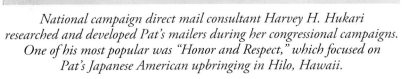

National campaign direct mail consultant Harvey H. Hukari researched and developed Pat's mailers during her congressional campaigns. One of his most popular was "Honor and Respect," which focused on Pat's Japanese American upbringing in Hilo, Hawaii.

*The king of Tonga, His Royal Highness Tafa'ahau Tupou IV,
accepts the gift of a porcelain American eagle from Pat at the Royal Palace
in Nuku'alofa. Pat led a presidential delegation to Tonga to mark the
100th anniversary of the Treaty of Friendship between the U.S.
and Tonga, as well as the king's 70th birthday.*

The Saiki ohana (family) poses in the backyard of the family home in Honolulu. From left, seated: son Stuart; daughter Margaret, DVM; Pat's father, Kazuo Fukuda; Pat; mother Shizue Fukuda; son Stanley Jr., MD; daughter Laura. Standing: husband Stanley, MD, and daughter Sandra, MD.

Pat speaks at a ceremony on the south side of the U.S. Capitol marking approval of a bill to provide a national apology and reparations for the internment of Japanese Americans during World War II. Pat played a crucial role in the bill's passage in the House of Representatives, where there were enough Republican "no" votes to keep the legislation bottled up in the House. Pat personally worked the GOP caucus and convinced enough members to vote for the bill that passage was ensured.

PART III ENDNOTES

1 That remained the case until November 2010, when Charles Djou, then a Republican who had won a special election in May 2010 to fill the U.S. House seat vacated by Neil Abercrombie, lost to Democrat Colleen Hanabusa.

2 Cecil Heftel: https://history.house.gov/People/Listing/H/HEFTEL,-Cecil-Landau-(H000449)/.

3 Prior to running for Congress, Heftel was a "multimillionaire broadcasting executive." Floyd K. Takeuchi, "Congressional battle fierce for 2 elections in 1," *Honolulu Star-Bulletin and Advertiser*, September 14, 1986.

4 Gregg K. Kakesako, "GOP's Patricia Saiki in U.S. House Race," *Honolulu Star-Bulletin*.

5 Hiram Fong served nearly two decades as one of Hawaii's first U.S. senators. He was the first person of Chinese descent elected to Congress, the first Asian Pacific American elected to the Senate and the first Chinese American candidate for the presidency, and he remains the only Republican senator ever elected from Hawaii. https://history.house.gov/People/Detail/15032451315

6 William F. Quinn was the last appointed governor of the territory of Hawaii and the first elected governor of the state of Hawaii. https://www.nytimes.com/2006/08/31/obituaries/31quinn.html

7 Mufi Hannemann: https://ballotpedia.org/Mufi_Hannemann.

8 Louis K. "Buzzy" Agard Jr.: https://obits.staradvertiser.com/2016/01/03/louis-k-buzzy-agard-jr/.

9 Floyd K. Takeuchi, "Congressional battle fierce for 2 elections in 1," *Honolulu Star-Bulletin and Advertiser,* September 14, 1986.

10 *Honolulu Star-Bulletin and Advertiser*, September 14, 1986

11 Congress adjourned on October 18, https://history.house.gov/Institution/Session-Dates/All/

12 "Saiki is Only Republican to Win Support of Teachers' Union" (undated clip).

13 Saiki won the general election with 59 percent of the vote, a 33,000-vote advantage; no previous Hawaiian Republican candidate for the U.S. House had ever polled more than 45 percent of the vote. https://history.house.gov/People/Detail/21149

14 John Christensen, "For Congresswoman-Elect Patricia Saiki, the Job Began as the Campaign Ended," *Honolulu Advertiser*, November 6, 1986.

15 Tom Horton, "U.S. Rep Pat Saiki: New Congresswoman in the Limelight," *Spirit of Aloha* magazine, July/August 1987.

16 Koa, a type of wood, grows predominantly on the Big Island of Hawaii.

17 In 1986 the Supreme Court ruled the Act unconstitutional on the grounds that the sequestration process gave Congress undue budgetary power. In 1987 the Act was passed again (see Gramm-Rudman-Hollings II), with a new sequestration process and deficit numbers; the revised legislation also pushed back the date the budget was to be balanced to 1993. https://bancroft.berkeley.edu/ROHO/projects/debt/1985grammrudmanhollings.html and https://www.encyclopedia.com/history/united-states-and-canada/us-history/gramm-rudman-hollings-act

18 Members of Congress are authorized by law to nominate candidates for appointment to four U.S. service academies. These schools are the U.S. Military Academy, the U.S. Naval Academy, the U.S. Air Force Academy and the U.S. Merchant Marine Academy. The fifth service academy, the U.S. Coast Guard Academy, does not require a congressional nomination for appointment. These institutions prepare college-age Americans to be officers of the U.S. uniformed services. Upon graduation, service academy graduates are commissioned as officers in the active or reserve components of the military or merchant marine for a minimum of five years. https://fas.org/sgp/crs/misc/RL33213.pdf.

19 Tom Horton, "U.S. Rep Pat Saiki: New Congresswoman in the Limelight," *Spirit of Aloha* magazine, July/August 1987.

20 U.S. Fishery Management Council: http://www.fisherycouncils.org/.

21 Frank Kunio Goto: (undated) https://obits.staradvertiser.com/2019/11/03/frank-kunio-goto/.

22 Brooks Takenaka: https://www.linkedin.com/in/brooks-takenaka-1b80ba9/.

23 Kitty Simonds: https://www.fisheries.noaa.gov/national/partners/council-contacts#pacific-fishery-management-council.

24 Walter Beaman Jones Sr. (August 19, 1913–September 15, 1992) was an American Democratic politician from the state of North Carolina who served in the U.S. House of Representatives from 1966 until his death. https://history.house.gov/People/Detail/16016

25 Transcript of President Reagan's speech: http://www.cnn.com/2005/ALLPOLITICS/01/31/sotu.reagan1985.3/index.html.

26 The "Reagan Doctrine": https://www.history.com/this-day-in-history/the-reagan-doctrine-is-announced.

27 Filadelfo Aleman, "Nicaragua Stifles Dissent, Closes Newspaper," *Honolulu Star-Bulletin*, June 27, 1986.

28 Michael T. Kaufman, "King Tafaahau Tupou IV, Ruler of Tonga, Dies at 88," *The New York Times*, September 11, 2006, https://www.nytimes.com/2006/09/11/world/asia/11tonga.html.

29 James Kelly continued to serve our country with distinction during President George W. Bush's administration as one of our top Asia experts.

30 Now called the Westin Denarau Island Resort and Spa, according to a New Zealand travel company website: https://www.ourpacific.co.nz/our-resorts/fiji/The-Westin-Denarau-Island-Resort-and-Spa.aspx.

31 The crown prince would become King George Tupou V when he succeeded his father in 2006.

32 Now called Tanoa International Dateline Hotel.

33 Colonel Thomas Wood: https://prabook.com/web/colonel.wood/518297.

34 David Hawkings, "Bob Michel, Last Leader of the 'Old School' House GOP, dies at 93," Roll Call, February 17, 2017. https://www.rollcall.com/2017/02/17/bob-michel-last-leader-of-the-old-school-house-gop-dies-at-93/.

35 Civil Liberties Act of 1987: https://www.congress.gov/bill/100th-congress/house-bill/442.

36 On April 21, 1945, Lt. Inouye was leading a flanking attack on a heavily defended ridge near San Terenzo in Tuscany, Italy. As he raised himself up and cocked his arm to throw his last grenade, a German soldier inside the bunker fired a rifle grenade, which struck his right elbow, nearly severing most of his arm and leaving his primed grenade reflexively "clenched in a fist that suddenly didn't belong to me anymore." The remainder of Inouye's mutilated right arm was later amputated at a field hospital and without proper anesthesia, as he had been given too much morphine at an aid station and it was feared any more would lower his blood pressure enough to kill him. He had to endure his arm being sawed off without anesthesia. https://www.nps.gov/articles/inouyeww2.htm.

37 Richard Borreca, "Saiki has slight edge in fund-raising battle," *Honolulu Star-Bulletin*, September 6, 1988.

38 The brochure includes a quote by state Senator Neil Abercrombie derived from the Senate Journal, March 31, 1983, page 474: "...why didn't the so-called consumer protector, Mrs. Bitterman, recommend changes in the law…so that these people could be protected…" and points out that "Fourteen lawsuits have been filed against Mary Bitterman as the result of her performance as the Director of the Department of Commerce and Consumer Affairs." On December 15, 1983, the brochure text continues, "Mary Bitterman resigns her position as Director and leaves state government."

39 The national legislature of Japan: https://www.britannica.com/topic/Diet-Japanese-government.

40 Karl Schoenberger, "World Leaders Pay Respects at Hirohito Rites: The Funeral of Emperor Hirohito," *Los Angeles Times*, February 24, 1989, https://www.latimes.com/archives/la-xpm-1989-02-24-mn-273-story.html.

41 Richard Cavendish, "Emperor Hirohito's State Funeral," *History Today* 64, no. 2 (2014), https://www.historytoday.com/archive/emperor-hirohito's-state-funeral.

42 Jim Borg, "Johnston weapons numbers rise: Chemical arms disposal weight vastly underestimated," *Honolulu Star Bulletin and Advertiser*, April 8, 1990.

43 Hawaii newspapers called for his resignation, intimating that he might be unable to properly represent the interests of the state. Matsunaga waved off the concerns as "trying to make a decision a little too soon."

44 While seeking treatment in Toronto, Matsunaga died on April 15, 1990. https://history.house.gov/People/Detail/17633.

45 Kahoolawe: http://kahoolawe.hawaii.gov/history.shtml.

46 RIMPAC is a multinational maritime exercise staged in and around the Hawaiian Islands. https://www.public.navy.mil/surfor/Pages/Rimpac-2018.aspx

47 For many years, this issue was in the public spotlight. On January 4, 1976, a group later called "The Kahoolawe Nine" defied restrictions and attempted to land on the island. Grassroots organizations including Protect Kahoolawe Ohana followed, with a series of island occupations and attempts to halt the bombing through lawsuits in the U.S. Federal District Court. The Hawaiian people even organized a group called "Stop the Bombing of Kahoolawe," led by the mayor of Maui, Hannibal Tavares, but to no avail. The effort to stop the bombing dragged on for years and years.

48 Ken Miller, "11 Pacific leaders to meet Bush," *Honolulu Star-Bulletin*, October 26, 1990.

49 Pacific Islands Development Program: https://www.forumsec.org/pacific-islands-development-program-pidp/.

*As Administrator of the U.S. Small Business Administration,
Pat tours the devastation on Kauai in September 1992 after
Hurricane Iniki slammed into the Hawaiian island.*

PART IV

The Small Business Administration Years and a Final Run for Office 1991–1994

Summoned by the President

A few weeks after the U.S. Senate race, my daughter Laura answered the phone one day while I was cooking breakfast at our family home in Honolulu. "Mom," she said. "The president wants to talk to you."

"Which president?" I asked. She went back on the phone to pose the question and returned with the answer: "the president of the United States, Mom."

That was the beginning of a whole new adventure in government. President George H. W. Bush wanted me to return to Washington, D.C., to head up the department or agency of my choice. He offered several options, but I immediately selected the U.S. Small Business Administration because small business was then, and remains, the backbone of our state's economy. Ninety-five percent of businesses in

Hawaii are considered small businesses.[1]

I felt confident that I was qualified to be the Administrator of this agency, which was founded in 1953 to assist, counsel and champion the interests of small business. My experience serving actively on the Banking, Finance and Urban Affairs Committee while in Congress made me familiar with the national impact the federal government had on all business, especially small business. I had never owned or run a small business, but I had enjoyed the privilege of serving on the board of directors for two of the most powerful businesses in my state.

Amfac, Inc., under its chairman—and my mentor—Henry Walker, was the biggest sugar producer in Hawaii, with diversified ownership of retail businesses including the Liberty House department stores. Tourism and real estate holdings included major resorts at Kaanapali (Maui) and Keauhou (the Big Island of Hawaii), as well as golf courses on the mainland. Amfac ran other agricultural businesses, producing potatoes, for example, which were sold to McDonald's and other fast food restaurants for making french fries. I was on the Amfac board for 13 years and held key positions, including serving on committees on nominations, compensation and audit.

My service on the board for Hawaiian Airlines, under CEO Jack Magoon, deepened my exposure to the travel industry. I enjoyed my 13 years of frontline involvement as the airline grew from a local carrier to one extending its reach to the mainland U.S. For that board, I served on committees on compensation and nominations.

When I became a member of the U.S. Congress, I had to vacate both boards. Nevertheless, the privilege and knowledge I gained while serving in these capacities made me very much aware of what the private-sector business environment was all about.

My husband Stanley and I returned to Washington, D.C., to the home we owned in Alexandria, Virginia, when I served in Congress. My purpose now was to achieve confirmation as Administrator of the SBA by the U.S. Senate.

I knew what the responsibilities involved. The agency was made up of nearly 4,000 employees spread across the whole of the United States, including Hawaii and the territory of Guam—ten regions with more than 100 offices. The SBA budget was $382 million, with loan authorization of almost $6 billion.[2] The loan portfolio at the time was about $23 billion, which was greater than that of most major banks.

But the agency's reputation was not so positive, and its leadership was considered something of a revolving door: Six administrators had served in the previous ten years. There was skepticism in the minds of the senators responsible for confirmation. Some felt the agency should be scrapped and the responsibility to assist small businesses be placed elsewhere.[3]

Some viewed the job as a consolation prize populated by defeated senatorial candidates. My predecessor, Susan Engeleiter, a former Wisconsin legislator, had made an unsuccessful bid for a U.S. Senate seat in her state. (She held the job for two years before leaving to take a job in private industry.) Her predecessor, James Abdnor, a former Republican senator from South Dakota, lost his seat in 1986.

My experience as a colleague and former member of Congress saved the day. My performance as a thoughtful leader gave skeptics reason to retain the organization and give it another try.

The Senate confirmation hearing was run by Senator Dale Bumpers, a Democrat from Arkansas and chairman of the Committee on Small Business.

It was held in the Russell Senate Office Building on March 20, 1991. Opening statements by Hawaii's congressional delegation—Senators Daniel Inouye and Daniel Akaka, and Representatives Neil Abercrombie and Patsy Mink, all in support of my candidacy, were impressive.

Supportive statements by state leaders—Governor John Waihee and Richard Wong, president of the Hawaii State Senate—also were entered into the record. Favorable testimony from my former colleagues in the U.S. House of Representatives—Nancy Johnson of Connecticut, Jan Meyer of Kansas, Marge Roekema of New Jersey, Barbara Vucanovic of Nevada, Olympia Snowe of Maine, Helen

Bentley of Maryland, Susan Molinari of New York, and Connie Mack and Ileana Ros-Lehtinen of Florida—gave me credibility. Statements presented by members of the committee—Senators Dixon, Baucus, Burns and Lieberman—were all favorable. Others had submitted written testimony expressing their support.

Of course I also had a stamp of approval from President Bush, who, while speaking to the Federation of Independent Businesses, touted the fact that I would be the first Asian American to hold this position and therefore especially helpful in understanding minority business interests.

During my own testimony, I promised to be a "hands-on, no-nonsense, results-oriented, can-do manager." I pledged to improve efficiency across all of the agency's general support programs and address communications issues that prevented many small businesses from taking advantage of services the SBA had to offer.[4]

The vote of the Small Business Committee was unanimous, though not without its jabs. "You're the third defeated senatorial candidate to head up the SBA," said Committee Chairman Bumpers. Still, he urged me to stay in the post, which he called "one of the toughest in government, and perhaps one of the most thankless."[5]

Soon after, on April 10, 1991, my entire family—all five children and my husband, Stanley—joined me in the Roosevelt Room in the West Wing of the White House as President Bush did me the honor of being first to congratulate me.

"Pat Saiki will be bringing her own spirit of aloha to this job," he said in a prepared statement. "And for those of you who don't know what I mean, just watch. Watch how she does over there. You talk about enthusiasm and ability, you're going to see it all—all at once." He described the SBA as "vitally important" and the nation's 20 million small business owners as "the heart of the American dream." I was moved when he described me as someone who would be a "tough, smart advocate" for small business owners. "I know her," he concluded, "and I know she'll throw her whole energy and dedication into this challenge because Pat will be responsible for more than administration and policy development. She's going to have the chance to help people shape their own futures."[6]

My son Stanley Jr. held the Bible as I was officially sworn in by U.S. Supreme Court justice Sandra Day O'Connor, who had kindly agreed, at my request, to do the honors.

Thus began one of the most exciting experiences and challenges of my career. It did not escape me that I was also the first person from Hawaii to serve as the head of a federal agency. This was a tremendous honor and I felt compelled to succeed.

It was daunting to face a nationwide staff of nearly 4,000 long-term civil servants. Most had been appointed by leaders of the Democrat Party. I knew that in order to accomplish anything positive, I would need a loyal personal staff, and I would have to win the loyalty of those already committed to their jobs. I also knew I had to work to alleviate the anxieties of people inside and outside of the organization who feared for its future.

I brought with me some of my congressional and long-serving loyal staff, including Bob Wernet [7] and Carolyn Lee from Hawaii, along with Anne Stanley, whom I appointed chief of staff, and Aileen Kishaba, a program specialist, both of whom had worked on my state legislative staff. I also had the opportunity to work with many outstanding public servants at SBA.

Among this exceptionally talented group was my New England regional director, Susan Collins of Maine. She and I worked closely together, and I was so impressed by her knowledge and commitment to public service that I urged Susan to consider running for Congress. It pleased me greatly when she did run, and today Susan is Senator Collins, the senior U.S. senator from Maine.

My first meeting with the agency's rank-and-file Washington, D.C., staff was a memorable one. Everyone looked apprehensive as I approached them with a big "Aloha!" from Hawaii. It seemed to soften the atmosphere and set the stage for my next announcement, which really won them over.

In Hawaii, every Friday was known as Aloha Friday, when all

workers were allowed to dress less formally and could set their jackets aside for aloha shirts or shirt sleeves for men. Women could substitute sandals for hose and heels. I declared that we would adopt the local custom in Washington and every Friday would be Aloha Friday at the SBA. My announcement was applauded with enthusiasm and adopted immediately.

Word got out to other agencies in D.C. and I received calls from cabinet heads including Lynn Martin, with whom I served when we were both in Congress and who was now the secretary of labor, along with others who followed suit and adopted our aloha spirit. They called it Casual Friday and I understand it is still observed today.

My Partner—Stanley M. Saiki, MD

I wanted to familiarize myself with the many regions of the SBA family and begin to build meaningful relationships with staff, so I immediately launched a series of visits to various state offices. Three weeks into my new job, I was in Florida when I received the devastating news that my husband, Stanley, had been taken to a hospital in Alexandria.

I had lived with constant fear about Stanley's health for many years. He had a longstanding condition that affected his heart and blood circulation and had undergone four coronary bypass procedures and a femoral artery bypass. He had retired from medical practice to accompany me to Washington when I was first elected to Congress in 1986. Since then, I had lived with the reality that any day could be his last.

Our son Stuart, who had a job in Washington, D.C., and lived with us, attended to his father when I was out of town, and it was Stuart who found his father at the end. When Stuart left for work on the morning of May 1, 1991, Stanley had finished breakfast and was sitting in his favorite chair, reading his newspaper. When Stuart came back home after work and called out to announce his return, his father didn't answer. Stuart found his father, sitting immobile in his chair, still holding his newspaper, and immediately summoned an ambulance. Stanley, just 73, was already gone.

Stanley was a surgeon and specialist in obstetrics and gynecology, and he had a successful private practice in Honolulu. He was known for his accomplishments as chief of obstetrics at Kapiolani Hospital for Women and was an active participant with the Honolulu County and state medical associations. He supported the successful—and only—emergency medical services program in Honolulu. It was my husband, along with Richard Davi, chief of staff at Kapiolani Hospital, who originally proposed the Sex Abuse Treatment Center at the hospital to give assistance and medical attention to women who were raped or otherwise abused.

We had a close relationship—we shared both personal and professional interests and for many years enjoyed playing golf together every weekend. We ended each day with our own version of "pillow talk," sharing the events of the day and advice on the respective challenges we faced. To lose my partner, mentor, trusted advisor and dependable spouse was a shock difficult to bear. We brought him home to Hawaii to be buried with an impressive memorial service at the beautiful Cathedral of St. Andrew in downtown Honolulu, attended by many patients, fellow physicians, family and friends, in addition to many of the people I had worked with while in the state legislature. Well-known local singer Melveen Leed[8] graciously performed Stanley's favorite song, "Wind Beneath My Wings," which gave me great comfort.

My five children—Stanley Jr., who was born in Philadelphia while his father was earning his specialty degree; daughters Sandra and Margaret, born in Toledo, Ohio, while their father was doing residency training in obstetrics/gynecology; Stuart and Laura, born in Honolulu when Stanley was in medical practice and I taught at Kaimuki Intermediate and Kalani High schools—gave me the strength and stability to continue my mission in public service.

With my husband's funeral over, and after taking a little time for adjustment and the realization of widowhood, I returned to Washington, D.C., to continue leading the SBA.

Communication, "Cockroaching" and Criticism

Communication was a major internal issue among staff at our regional offices. Our Office of Information and Communications division pointed out that differing computer systems in the ten regions were part of the problem. To me, this was inexplicable. Why couldn't all regions use one uniform computerized system?

The Office of Information had made numerous requests to overhaul our computer system and bring everything under one umbrella, but the decision kept being postponed. Ready excuses included lack of funds and staff resistance to new ways and additional training.

Because communication is the basis for efficiency in any organization, I quickly vowed to tackle this issue. I developed a creative funding plan involving all the regions. I called it my "cockroach plan." The name raised a few eyebrows among my colleagues but made perfect sense to me: In pidgin English, "cockroach" is a verb used to describe taking something from another. I saw a solution in taking "a little bit from here, a little bit from there." Each region of the SBA assumed a portion of the cost of the unified network. New computer equipment and training recommended by our Office of Information in Washington finally could be purchased and installed. We moved quickly and succeeded against all possible bureaucratic obstacles. It did marvelous things to improve the effectiveness of the agency and the morale of personnel.

This effort to harness our computer communication effort led to the development of SBA ONLINE, a national, small business electronic bulletin board providing immediate access to information, programs and services available to the public through our agency.

Another basic, but serious, situation was resolved when I requested a meeting with the new secretary of defense, Dick Cheney, with whom I had the pleasure of serving while we were both in the Congress. It was rumored that he would be less strict about an existing congressional mandate that ten percent of all defense contracts be given to minority entities. I wanted assurances that minority-owned small businesses would continue to benefit from that mandate.

During a friendly meeting at the Pentagon, Secretary Cheney told me minority-owned businesses would continue to be issued contracts as stipulated by Congress. This gave our SBA officers much relief, and the motivation they needed to implement this important policy. After all, ten percent of all defense contracts is a magnificent boost to small business.

It then came to my attention that I should look into conditions in my own state. I had heard rumors that small businesses in Hawaii, which depend on local banks for financing, were not benefitting from SBA support as much as they should.

After investigating, I learned that the director of the Hawaii SBA office was looking forward to retirement—and not acting as aggressively as he could have been to implement available programs. According to the Civil Service Reform Act of 1968,[9] civil service employees can be fired only for blatant misconduct, poor performance or medical inability to perform.[10] I couldn't fire someone for mere lack of interest in the job. So I offered the director a relocation to Alaska, where he could enjoy a different climate and venue while he waited out his retirement. We both knew my "offer" was not negotiable. He immediately chose early retirement, which opened the prospect of new management in Hawaii.

Under federal law, I had to consider anyone interested in seeking the job. But all applicants faced the same hurdles: a battery of tests and a scoring system that ranks candidates in eight categories, including administrative background, financial background, overseas marketing experience and managing people.[11]

An all-out national search ensued, resulting in three applicants who scored in the top three. These three moved forward in the hiring process.

The candidate with the highest score was Andrew Poepoe, a close friend and a respected former state legislator with whom I'd served. Poepoe, who held executive positions with the Dole Packaged Foods company for more than 25 years before entering politics,[12] was eminently qualified. I knew his talents and experiences would make a good fit for the SBA position.

It was my pleasure to appoint Poepoe to the position of district administrator for the SBA in Hawaii. He proved to be a dynamo, awakening the Hawaii business community and offering entrepreneurs access to capital. He earned the respect of the banking community and worked closely with our D.C. office and other regions.

All of this was taking place in the midst of a national economic downturn, which was almost as bad as a recession. Regional banks were failing, which meant the elimination of credit and loans. Small businesses in these areas were facing closure. Hardest hit were those in the New England states.

The situation prompted creation of the New England Recovery Plan administered by Mitchell Stanley, the SBA deputy associate administrator for finance, investment and procurement.[13] This SBA-guaranteed loan program stabilized credit, helped maintain jobs and expanded employment for small businesses. The concept quickly spread throughout New England and into other regions suffering the same conditions.

I took some criticism for launching the program in New England. President Bush was seeking a second term, and New England would be pivotal to his reelection campaign. I weathered attacks by Democrat congressmen from the area because I felt strongly that the importance of stabilizing local banks far exceeded the sting of political attacks I would have to endure. We went ahead with our plans—and succeeded in revitalizing the economy.

Another priority had first come to my attention more than two decades earlier, when I served as a member of President Richard Nixon's Citizens Advisory Council on the Status of Women.[14] Women entrepreneurs sorely needed assistance getting started. We expanded the Office of Women's Business Ownership to include counseling, marketing support and seminars on securing credit and government contracts.

I focused on a microloan program for women who sought funding to start small businesses. Most of these women wanted to start businesses out of their homes; the amount of seed capital they needed was small. Our finance group developed and put into motion a program that provided entrepreneurs the funding they needed to enter the small business market. This effort to encourage more women to become independent owners proved both popular and successful.

Then, in the midst of attempting new and necessary programs to help solve banking problems created by the recession, we were slammed by two major natural disasters.

The Hurricanes

Hurricane Andrew hit Florida on August 28, 1992, and Hurricane Iniki struck Hawaii on September 11. Our agency immediately was called to action to assist small businesses devastated by these back-to-back disasters.

In Florida, 61 people were killed by the Category 5 hurricane and damages mounted to the tune of $27 billion. I flew over affected parts of Florida to view the wreckage and began coordinating the recovery effort. Less than a month later, I got a call from the White House requesting that I head immediately to Andrews Air Force Base. A military jet was ready to fly me and the head of the Federal Emergency Management Agency to attend to the damage Hurricane Iniki inflicted on the Hawaiian Islands—specifically the island of Kauai, 108 miles northwest of Oahu. It was shocking, while flying over this island known for its open sugarcane fields and impeccable beaches, to see the devastation caused by winds clocking 145 miles per hour.

The local airport was closed because of the storm, so we could not land our aircraft on Kauai and had to fly back to Honolulu. There, Andrew Poepoe, the SBA district administrator I had appointed, sought help from his friend, Major General Edward Richardson, who was in charge of the Hawaii National Guard. General Richardson arranged for a national guard aircraft to fly us from Wheeler Field in Wahiawa, to Lihue, Kauai. The propeller aircraft was filled with MREs (meals ready to eat) for the people of Kauai. When we arrived, we were joined by SBA Disaster Administrator Berkie Kulick[15] and our local SBA staff, who worked efficiently to provide help.

Iniki, which means "strong and piercing wind" in Hawaiian, was designated a Category 4 storm[16]—the most powerful to hit the islands in recorded history, and the most costly.

Residents simply were not prepared for this storm. Many had gone about their usual business the day before it hit, confident it would bypass them because of its straightforward trajectory far south of the islands. That Thursday, people were at work. Children were at school. More than 100 cast and crew members, including director Steven Spielberg, were wrapping up filming for the first *Jurassic Park* movie. But by late that afternoon, the storm took an unexpected sharp turn north. Residents were shocked when the hurricane warning was announced about 8:30 that night. By midnight, JoAnn Yukimura— Kauai's mayor at the time—had activated the Emergency Operations Center.[17]

The hit to Kauai was direct and the damage to the homes and businesses amounted to approximately $1.8 billion in 1992 dollars. The people—and small businesses—needed help to recover.

We paid an official visit to Kauai County headquarters and met with Mayor Yukimura, who had slept on the floor of her office when the hurricane hit.[18]

She was triaging multiple crises—restoring clean water supplies and electricity, diverting trash and circumventing communication blackouts while telephone lines were down. Residents and officials sent messages by bicycle, ham radio or over the airwaves of local radio station KONG. As supplies came in from U.S. military bases on Guam, a new concern arose: making sure none of the planes carried stowaways, the brown tree snakes that had wreaked so much damage on that tiny island. Yukimura worried that an infestation of brown tree snakes would be more damaging to the island than Iniki itself had been.[19]

As we met with small business owners whose livelihoods were destroyed by the storm, I recognized how isolated they felt. As residents on an island distanced from the mainland by time and geography, they needed easier access to funding assistance. To speed up the loan approval process, I asked personnel from the Department of the Treasury and the Internal Revenue Department to set up disaster-relief offices in Honolulu. After shaking many bureaucratic cages, my request was approved and personnel were flown over from the mainland, some handcuffed to briefcases containing millions of dollars. We set up a secure office in Honolulu where they could safely and efficiently disburse funds to hurricane victims.

Earlier that year, another traumatic incident had required our services. Many small businesses needed recovery assistance after the April 1992 riots in Los Angeles, which erupted after the acquittal of four white Los Angeles Police Department officers in the beating of black motorist Rodney King in 1991.[20]

Through each of these challenges, my focus remained on revitalizing the SBA's core programs to facilitate access to capital for small business growth and development across the country. Fortunately, I realized the full support of Congress. Small business loans in 1992 increased by 35 percent over the prior year. Loans to export businesses increased by a whopping 95 percent. We overhauled the Small Business Investment Company program to play a major role in venture capital financing.[21]

The 1992 Republican National Convention was held August 17–20 that year at the Astrodome in Houston, Texas.[22] Ronald Reagan gave his last major public address, Pat Buchanan fired up the crowd and HIV activist Mary Fischer, herself a victim of the virus, spoke movingly about the epidemic then facing our country.[23] I had the privilege and honor to serve as an official seconder to the nomination of President George H. W. Bush.

But when the November elections rolled around, Bush lost his bid for a second term as president. His loss was blamed in part on slow recovery from the national financial crisis that occurred during his first term.

As a political appointee, my time at the SBA came to a halt. For me it was a sorry day, for it meant the dissolution of an effective team of talented and dedicated people who had made tremendous contributions to help small businesses across our nation.

Harvard University

My political friends in Hawaii, especially state senator Andy Anderson, realized I would now be free to pursue new political endeavors. They immediately called to ask me to consider running for governor and head the Republican ticket. Many people encouraged me to consider the campaign. Party officials endorsed the idea and asked me to return to the islands.

As luck and timing would have it, I was also approached about taking a one-semester teaching position at the John F. Kennedy School of Government at Harvard University. The teacher in me saw this as an opportunity to work in a very special environment and to return, at least temporarily, to a career I had enjoyed very much. After all, how many people get an offer like this? The prestigious Kennedy School is dedicated to improving public policy and leadership in the United States and around the world.[24] I couldn't turn it down, even as my dear Republican friends pressured me to return to Hawaii to start organizing for what would be a difficult and challenging race for governor.

The election was two years away. I figured I could teach the spring 1993 semester at Harvard then return home to plan for the 1994 campaign. Hoping my friends would understand, I accepted the Harvard challenge. I went to Cambridge and became an Institute of Politics Visiting Fellow at the Harvard Kennedy School. When I got to campus, I was delighted to discover that my U.S. House colleague, Lynn Martin, a Republican who represented Illinois in Congress and then served as secretary of labor when I ran the SBA, was also a Visiting Fellow.

I was given free rein in designing my course, which involved government, politics and business. It encouraged dialogue on many current issues and was open to both graduate and undergraduate students. My classes were very well attended, and the student response was enthusiastic.

Discussions were vigorous, with student opinions ranging from the very liberal to the very conservative. I shared my experiences as a legislator, explaining how I made decisions to amend laws to solve difficult financial and social problems. My students relished the personal touch and context my anecdotes provided and were full of questions and arguments. The experience was invigorating for us all.

One of the most exciting aspects of being on campus was exposure to so many talented and educated professors from various parts of our country and the world. I was encouraged to meet with these educators and could attend their courses at my pleasure.

One professor from Japan was especially interesting to me and I attended some of his classes because the subject intrigued me. It was about the time in history when Japan was moving from segmented regional banks (involving credit banks, trust banks, mutual loan and savings banks) to more centralized and organized institutions that could provide broader services to clients, allowing them to expand their businesses and include foreign investments. During this time Japan rose to become home to one of the five largest banking institutions in the world. I suppose my involvement as a member of the Committee on Finance and Banking while in Congress laid the foundation for my curiosity. I found the lectures by this Japanese philosopher fascinating.

Weekly luncheons with other educators were opportunities to exchange ideas, philosophies and even biases. There were many social events, which I appreciated. It all broadened my perspectives and allowed time to get to know others involved in top-level education.

Frank Luntz [25] was a Kennedy School Visiting Fellow at the same time. He was working even then to organize and perfect a public forum style of polling, involving Harvard students in developing techniques that led him to a successful career as a pollster, pundit and political consultant. In 2008, he founded Luntz Global Partners, which he left in 2017.[26] Today, he makes frequent television appearances on Fox News as a commentator and analyst and runs focus groups during and after presidential debates. He also has authored three *New York Times* best-selling books on messaging and public opinion.[27]

My work life at Harvard was most fulfilling, but the weather in Boston in the spring was not exactly what I was accustomed to. Snow up to one's knees for months at a time was difficult for someone from Hawaii. I spent the weekdays in Boston but always hurried back to my Arlington, Virginia, home on the weekends. I learned much about commuting on trains.

The Race for Governor of Hawaii

When my term as a resident scholar at Harvard came to a close, it was time to come home to Hawaii and settle into another challenge. The race for governor was still hot on the agenda of my friends, who had waited patiently for me to begin serious discussions on mounting a major campaign.

Lieutenant Governor Ben Cayetano would be running on the Democrat side and there was much speculation that former Honolulu mayor Frank Fasi would run as an independent on his own Best Party ticket. Here was a colorful, popular politician, often called a maverick, who more often than not performed as an independent.

On November 4, a full year before the election, the press issued results of a poll asking, "If the election for governor were held today, which candidate would you vote for?" Results showed 16 percent for Fasi, 24 percent for Cayetano and 40 percent for me.

Before getting into the nitty-gritty of the race, let me digress and share a little history involving Frank Fasi.

Fasi was a longtime incumbent Democrat mayor who was defeated during the 1980 primary election. Democrat leaders, who always questioned Fasi's loyalties, abandoned him that year to support Eileen Anderson, a former Hawaiian Telephone Company (now Hawaiian Telcom) employee who had served in various state agencies, including a role as the state's first budget and finance director under Governor George Ariyoshi.

At that time, I was serving as chairman of the Republican Party of Hawaii. My friend and former state Senate colleague Andy Anderson, a creative and gifted pragmatist, convinced me we should solicit Frank to run for mayor against Eileen again in 1984, but this time as a Republican.

There was never any love lost between these two titans of Hawaii politics. Andy had run to unseat Frank as mayor on one occasion and on another they ran against each other for governor, which neither won.

But as we all know, "politics makes strange bedfellows." This was an opportunity to upset the political applecart: Frank Fasi could run to reinstate himself as Honolulu's mayor, but this time as a Republican with our party's support.

I had my reservations concerning this idea. I always considered Fasi to be sexist, one who didn't approve of women in high positions of leadership. His disdain for women only strengthened when he lost his longtime mayoral position to Anderson, a woman.

However, I had to put my personal feelings aside for possible political party gain. At Andy's urging, we invited Frank to consider this proposal. We managed to persuade him, and after a contentious election Frank once again became mayor.[28] He wisely convinced Andy to become his managing director. To this day, we enjoy the fruits of Andy Anderson's artistry and common sense. He was the architect of traffic light synchronization to improve traffic control. The best example of this is on King Street, a one-way street from downtown Honolulu to the University of Hawaii area in Manoa. If you start downtown and travel by car at 35 miles per hour, you will get directly through to the Manoa area (barring any accidents or other unforeseen disruptions), hitting green lights all the way.

Given all that history, I was facing a truly bizarre situation ten years later, as a candidate for governor against the Democrat Ben Cayetano on one side and this possible third-party candidate, Frank Fasi, on the other. Adding to the surreal nature of the situation, Andy Anderson—Fasi's former managing director—was helping manage my campaign.[29]

In politics, anytime there is a strong three-party race the outcome is totally unpredictable. I have to wonder if that was Fasi's intent—to throw the election into a "winner take all" situation. By splitting the votes, he could win, or at least prevent me from winning. He suddenly changed his liberal views and became very conservative, taking stances—against abortion, same-sex marriage, equal rights, etc.—that appealed to the most right wing of my supporters. Many of these conservative Republican voters abandoned me for Fasi.

There were charges against Fasi for unethical behavior involving campaign contributions and his unwillingness to play by the rules. One incident involved a public ad used both in print and on television, in which he attempted to smear Ben Cayetano by superimposing his face onto the face of former governor George Ariyoshi and my face onto the face of Andy Anderson—then morphing both of our faces into the face of Larry Mehau, a popular but controversial figure alleged to be the "godfather" of crime in Hawaii.[30]

This effort would backfire on Fasi, however, because Cayetano already had the backing of the Democrat "machine"—Democrats in party and legislative leadership plus leaders of the labor unions and government workers. This was to be expected. When you run against the ruling party, you are running against powerful agents who don't want their influence in government challenged.

I hoped that my years of experience and my record of serving various constituencies would be reminders to the voters that I cared about their future. I believed my consistent work on their behalf would supersede their loyalties to their union and organizational leaders. Maybe I was naïve, but I remained confident that individual voters would make individual decisions and vote their consciences.

My expectations did not match the outcome. When it comes time to vote, partisan politics, special interests and family loyalties always take precedence over individual thinking and personal observations. My effort was defeated by voters' overdependence on the status quo. Fasi was successful in splitting my vote and we both lost the election to Ben Cayetano, who won with just 36 percent of the vote.

In recalling this election, I must admit that my greatest disappointment was with many of the schoolteachers for whom I'd fought all of my legislative years.

The University of Hawaii professors and the HGEA (the government workers whose board of directors I had served) did not come through for me. They sided with union leaders looking to preserve their influence. It was a bitter pill to swallow.

The positive outcome was remembering the many warm endorsements I received and the exciting gatherings held with family and old friends. My special memory was time spent in Hilo, where I was born, raised and went to school. My cousin Alvin Inoue and his wife, Sharon Scheele Inoue, were helpful in launching my campaign in Hilo. Alvin was always there at the airport to pick me up and drive me to campaign events. The response from my Hilo High classmates, who held campaign signs on the streets, was heartwarming. Haru Yamane, chairman of the Hilo effort, set up a special headquarters and coordinated many campaign activities. Bea Isemoto was most active in my efforts to run for governor.

I remember a fundraiser organized by the politically controversial Big Island rancher Larry Mehau. To me, Larry was simply a classmate and a friend who supported me for governor and helped organize a very successful event where we gathered old and new friends in Hilo.

I will always be grateful for the endorsement and support of the prestigious Matsuura family of Hilo, including the former state senator David Matsuura, a Democrat, and his mother, Ruth Matsuura, a well-known and respected pediatrician. In her endorsement piece, Dr. Matsuura said, "The choice of who will be our next governor cannot be made simply by party affiliation. Thank heavens that in a democracy, we do have the freedom of choice. We are openly coming forth in favor of Pat Saiki for our next governor."

The prominent Democrat family of the late Kazuichi "Kazu" Sunada, who was closely aligned with Governor Jack Burns and the Hawaii Democratic Revolution of 1954,[31] also endorsed me. As his son Richard recalled, "Before he died, he brought the whole family together to ask us to do whatever to help elect Pat Saiki." In an endorsement flyer, the family wrote, "[Kazu] felt that Pat Saiki, more than any other candidate, would be able to bring all our people and views together in a harmonious fashion and lead us into the 21st century." These endorsements were humbling and will always be appreciated and remembered.

Many other prominent Hilo individuals endorsed my candidacy for governor. Among them were Mike Abe, a recognized leader in the Japanese American community. As he wrote in a piece for publication, "my decision to support Pat Saiki didn't come easily, but she is the only one who offers real hope. We've got to get the state moving and make some real changes."

Many other supporters throughout the state included stalwart Republicans who braved the pressures of Democrat dominance. I shall always be grateful for the help I received in this most challenging of races.

That wasn't the end of my involvement in Hawaii or Republican politics. In 2014, I came out of retirement to serve as interim chair for the Hawaii Republican Party, which was then in pretty bad shape. In a little over a year, with the help of a lot of friends and supporters—and the popularity and positive reputation of former governor Linda Lingle, who took the chairmanship of the party after her governorship and successfully increased our numbers in the state House to 19 out of 51 members—I was able to raise funds to encourage and help rebuild the party.

When I stepped down, I left the party with more than $200,000 in its bank account. This allowed the incoming chair, Fritz Rohlfing, to start with a clean slate. 🌿

*Former First Lady Barbara Bush, a close friend,
campaigned in Hawaii when Pat ran for governor in 1994.*

*Pat at the U.S. Small Business Administration with her friend
and SBA colleague Anne Stanley.*

*As Administrator of the U.S. Small Business Administration, Pat meets with
her governing council in Washington, D.C. From left to right, they are
Paul Cooksey, Dan Eramian, Gail McGrath, Anne Stanley, Pat,
Michael Wyatt, Mary Lukens, Mitchell Stanley and John Whitmore.*

*Former First Lady Barbara Bush campaigns in Hawaii for Pat
during the 1994 race for governor.*

To Pat
Best regards,

*Senator Bob Dole of Kansas was a close friend and colleague,
and Pat actively supported Dole's two runs for the presidency.*

*Pat is sworn in as Administrator of the U.S. Small Business Administration.
Her oldest son, Stanley Jr., holds the Bible, while President George H. W. Bush
looks on. Pat asked U.S. Supreme Court justice Sandra Day O'Connor
to administer the oath of office.*

Pat meets the national press outside of the White House after being sworn in as Administrator of the U.S. Small Business Administration. Dr. Stanley Saiki is at far left in a wheelchair being pushed by their son, Dr. Stanley Saiki, Jr.

Pat with supporters during her 1994 run for governor of Hawaii.

Dr. Stanley Saiki and Pat enjoy the cherry blossoms in Washington, D.C.

Andy Poepoe, Hawaii director of the U.S. Small Business Administration, drives Pat around Kauai as they inspect the damage inflicted by Hurricane Iniki in 1992.

*Pat boards a Harvard University bus during the semester she was invited
to teach at the John F. Kennedy School of Government.*

Pat with longtime friend Peter Tali Coleman,
former governor of American Samoa.

PART IV ENDNOTES

1   SBA definition of "small business" varies by industry. https://www.sba.gov/document/support-table-size-standards

2   "Choice of Saiki is good news for small business," *Honolulu Star-Bulletin*, March 13, 1991.

3   The Reagan administration, in fact, had moved to abolish it as an independent agency. https://www.chicagotribune.com/news/ct-xpm-1986-06-18-8602130574-story.html

4   Statistics from this time indicate that only one half of one percent of small businesses engaged in SBA activities.

5   "Saiki gets committee's OK," *Honolulu Advertiser*, March 21, 1991.

6   The White House Office of the Press Secretary, April 10, 1991, "Remarks by the President at Swearing-in Ceremony of Pat Saiki as Administrator of the Small Business Administration."

7   Robert "Bob" Wernet was a television journalist who served as Pat's press secretary during her second term when she was in the U.S. House. Prior to that, he had held the same position for Hawaii governor George Ariyoshi. http://the.honoluluadvertiser.com/article/2002/Jul/24/ln/ln63a.html

8   Melveen Leed: https://www.pbshawaii.org/long-story-short-with-leslie-wilcox-melveen-leed/.

9   Civil Service Reform Act of 1978: https://ballotpedia.org/Civil_Service_Reform_Act.

10 Joanna Friedman, "When can the federal government lawfully terminate employees?" Federal News Network, March 13, 2020, https://federalnewsnetwork.com/commentary/2020/03/when-can-the-federal-government-lawfully-terminate-employees/.

11 Mark Coleman, "It's a small, small world: Andrew Poepoe leads the federal government's small business efforts," *Honolulu Star-Bulletin*, December 27, 2004, http://archives.star-bulletin.com/2004/12/27/business/story1.html.

12 "Hawaii District Director of SBA plans to retire," *Honolulu Star-Bulletin*, December 4, 2008, says Poepoe was with Dole for just 25 years (1962-1988): http://archives.starbulletin.com/content/20081204_Hawaii_district_director_of_SBA_plans_to_retire "It's a small, small world: Andrew Poepoe leads the federal government's small business efforts," *Honolulu Star-Bulletin*, December 27, 2004, says "about 30 years." http://archives.star-bulletin.com/2004/12/27/business/ story1.html "SBA'S Poepoe plans to retire—again," *Honolulu Advertiser*, December 11, 2008: http://the.honoluluadvertiser.com/article/2008/Dec/11/bz/hawaii812110314.html.

13 "...positions in the Federal government involved organization of Federal resources to manage financial institutions regulatory issues at the Federal Home Loan Bank Board and as Deputy Administrator of SBA for Finance, Investment and Procurement where innovative solutions were needed to solve widespread problems in the banking and capital markets sectors." https://www.muuzii.com/about-us/management/
"... during Mr. Stanley's tenure with the Federal Government as Deputy Administrator of the U.S. Small Business Administration in charge of the SBA's Finance, Investment and Procurement programs; a portfolio of national programs designed to promote access to capital for small business and entrepreneurs and government contracts for qualified minority contractors (8A) during the early 1990's." https://bio.prlog.org/muuziinews/50005266-mitchell-stanley.html

14 UH timeline: In 1967 Pat became a member of the President's Citizens Advisory Council on the Status of Women.

15 "Bernard Kulik has been running the SBA's disaster assistance program for 12 years—long enough to earn the nickname 'Master of Disaster.'" Nancy Rivera Brooks, "Borrowing Trouble: Small-Firm Owners Still Awaiting SBA Quake Relief," *Los Angeles Times*, April 2, 1994, https://www.latimes.com/archives/la-xpm-1994-04-02-fi-41444-story.html.

16 In the south Pacific, the terms "typhoon," "tropical storm" or "tropical cyclone" are used to describe a rotating, organized system of clouds and thunderstorms. In most of the Atlantic and the northwest Pacific, the term "hurricane" is used to describe the same phenomenon. The main difference in describing the two types is location of origin (tropical storms originate over tropical or subtropical waters. The categories assigned differentiate wind speed, which helps predict levels of damage. Categories do not reflect expected amounts of rain or storm surge. https://oceanservice.noaa.gov/facts/cyclone.html and https://www.cnn.com/us/live-news/hurricaneflorencedle/h_adb70cdce0cfbb-9da1aef87c404da6e2.

17 Ashley Nagaoka, "It was the calm before the storm of Hurricane Iniki — and Kauai didn't know what it was in for," Hawaii News Now, September 10, 2017, https://www.hawaiinewsnow.com/story/36329839/25-years-ago-a- normal-day-turned-into-a-mad-scramble-as-iniki-turned-to-kauai/.

18 Jenna Carpenter, "JoAnn Yukimura remembers being mayor during Hurricane Iniki," *The Garden Island*, September 10, 2017, https://www.thegardenisland.com/2017/09/10/hawaii-news/joann-yukimura-remembers-being-mayor-during-hurricane-iniki/.

19 Yukimura's recollection from a 2017 story in *The Garden Island*, Kauai's newspaper since 1961.

20 LA riots: https://www.cnn.com/2013/09/18/us/los-angeles-riots-fast-facts/index.html.

21 Small Business Investment Company: https://www.sba.gov/funding-programs/investment-capital.

22 The convention ended eight days before Hurricane Andrew struck Florida on August 28. https://legacy.lib.utexas.edu/taro/ricewrc/00680/00680-P.html

23 https://www.youtube.com/watch?v=zB5K9k SOo.

24 Harvard Kennedy School: https://www.hks.harvard.edu/more/about.

25 A political and communications consultant, pollster and pundit best known for developing talking points and other messaging for Republican causes. "Luntz made his name by advising Republicans to repackage their policies with language designed to play more to emotion than intellect. He convinced conservatives to say they oppose a 'death tax' rather than an 'estate tax' on the inheritances of the wealthy, and urged the Bush administration to call global warming 'climate change.'" https://www.politico.com/story/2019/03/27/frank-luntz- trump-white-house-1238283

26 Frank Luntz: https://www.businesswire.com/news/home/20190924005709/en/Luntz-Global-Partners-Relaunches-Storyline-Strategies.

27 Pioneer of the "Instant Response" focus group technique, Frank has written, supervised and conducted more than 2,000 surveys, focus groups, and tests, and dial sessions in over two dozen countries and four continents over the past decade. Frank also has authored three *New York Times* best-selling books on messaging and public opinion. https://www.linkedin.com/in/frankluntz/.

28 Frank Fasi was the longest serving mayor in Honolulu, serving for a total of 22 years within the period 1969–2003. https://www.bizjournals.com/pacific/stories/2010/02/01/daily31.html.

29 Jerry Burris, "Frank 'n' Andy: There they go," *Honolulu Advertiser* editorial pages, May 8, 1994.

30 Steve Uyehara, "'The Goodfather' Dives into the Life of Larry Mehau," Hawaii News Now, May 17, 2018, https://www.hawaiinewsnow.com/story/38217078/the-goodfather-dives-into-life-of-larry-mehau/.

31 "The history of ethnic political divisions in Hawaii goes back to what's known as the Democratic Revolution of 1954, when Asian-American voters teamed up to take on the political power of Hawaii's white plantation owners. Young Japanese-American soldiers—including [Daniel] Inouye—returned home to Hawaii after World War II, went to college, and began running for office, culminating in the 1954 elections where Asian-American Democrats ousted many white Republican politicians." Emily Schultheis and National Journal, "How Ethnicity Weighs on Hawaii's Democratic Primary," *The Atlantic*, July 16, 2014, https://www.theatlantic.com/politics/archive/2014/07/how-ethnicity-weighs-on-hawaiis-democratic-primary/457914/.

*Pat took up sewing Hawaiian design quilts as a way to deal with stress.
She made one large quilt for each of her five children.*

PART V

Former Candidate, Private Citizen and Volunteer

After many years in public service, it was time to accept my role as a "former candidate and legislator," return to private sector life, reflect on my years of service and decide how to best continue that commitment as a volunteer.

My children, of course, were relieved that the pressures of serving the public were over and more of my time could be spent on family endeavors. I also had more freedom to enjoy exercise classes, improving my golf game and other personal interests I had always intertwined with my legislative career.

One pursuit in particular had always provided solace and diversion from the pressures and demands of my work. Inspired by my seamstress mother, I developed a passion for creative handiwork—crocheting, knitting, sewing and quilting.

Over my many years in politics, I embroidered tablecloths, table runners and doilies. I knitted sweaters, quilted pillows and wall hangings, and finished my big project of quilting five queen-size bedspreads for the five children to remember me by. I'd worked hard on these quilts and wanted to make sure they withstood the tests of time and wear. So, each quilt was delivered with a stern warning: Don't ever sit on the stitches and *never* let a cat walk on your quilt. I threatened to haunt them from the grave if they didn't follow my instructions!

My Favorite Years, as a Volunteer

Volunteerism has always been in my blood. As a parent, supporting the activities and efforts of my children was very important to me. I remember when the Kaimuki Intermediate School band needed to raise funds to participate in the Rose Parade in Pasadena, California.[1] The band teacher, Mr. Ben Kuraya, organized a group of us to form a fundraising team. We were delighted when our efforts meant the band could travel to proudly represent our state, wearing beautiful new uniforms, during the nationally televised parade.

It was during my teaching days that I got involved with my husband's cousin, Gilbert Saiki, a public school teacher in the field of special education. He and some fellow teachers were the original organizers of Hawaii's Special Olympics athletic events for children with disabilities.

At their request, I became chairman of what was then called the "Special Olympics for Retarded Children." (The word "retarded" would never be used today, of course, but in those days, it was commonly used to describe people with intellectual disabilities.) I arranged for competitions to be held on the athletic fields at Punahou School, where I'd started my teaching career.

I knew we had to form a nonprofit organization in order to legally raise money for the events, and I had good friends to join this effort: attorney Tom Rice and his wife, Phyllis, who were strong supporters. Tom drew up legal papers creating the nonprofit, allowing financial supporters to contribute with tax-deductible donations.

The new nonprofit joined with Eunice Kennedy's national initiative and expanded into the large, successful organization it is today. Many of Hawaii's children with disabilities have benefitted over the years from the efforts of that small founding group of teachers. It has been very satisfying to see these children compete and gain recognition for their participation in sports. I followed up this interest by becoming a director of the Variety Club School for Learning Disabilities.[2]

My interest in education continued in volunteer efforts as part of the governing board of Hawaii Pacific College and extended to the trusteeship of the University of Hawaii Foundation. I also served as a commissioner on the National Education Commission of the States. These positions built upon my earlier experience as a classroom teacher, and my later involvement with the Western Interstate Commission on Higher Education to provide educational opportunities for students in fields or professional tracks not available at our local university.

One of my proudest areas of volunteerism came during my state legislative years. As a member of the Medical Auxiliary of the Hawaii Medical Association, I learned this group was eager to get involved in supporting health-related legislation. Teaching them how laws were written, promoted and passed was like being in a classroom again— but this time with eager and involved adult students.

The Medical Auxiliary played an important role in filling communication gaps between legislators and physicians. Some of the women who participated in this effort went on to become effective lobbyists and headed other organizations promoting safety, including Carol McNamee, who in 1984 organized the Hawaii chapter of Mothers Against Drunk Driving.[3]

One of the leaders of the Auxiliary project was Miriam Hellreich, a practicing speech-language pathologist and fellow physician's wife. Miriam recognized the need for better state licensing requirements and accountability measures for speech-language pathologists and audiologists, who work with the hearing impaired. Miriam's insights and her expertise as a practitioner contributed greatly to the legislation we drafted, introduced and passed to license and regulate these professions.[4]

Miriam had a keen interest in and a passion for resolving problems through legislation, and she was relentless—just the kind of person we needed to get things done. I saw a future in harnessing her energy and her commitment to medical and health issues, and perhaps even broader political issues down the road. I recruited her to join the Hawaii Republican Party's efforts to elect more candidates to office. She worked her way into the Party and was elected in 1992 as national committeewoman representing Hawaii at the Republican National Committee.

She also serves as vice chair of the western region of the Republican National Committee and is on the executive committee of the RNC.[5]

Miriam is an effective fundraiser who worked on Governor Linda Lingle's successful 2002 campaign and served as finance director for the governor's 2006 reelection campaign.[6] Four years later, Miriam served as finance director for James R. "Duke" Aiona's 2010 race for governor.[7] The Hawaii Republican Party's candidates still count on her for advice and counsel on how to raise campaign funds.

One of Miriam's significant achievements was to serve as chair of the capital campaign to help pay off the mortgage on the party headquarters on Kapiolani Boulevard in Honolulu. Martha Daniels, a loyal member of the League of Republican Women, had left a sizable contribution in her will to be used as a down payment, but it was Miriam, with the help of the Oahu League of Republican Women, who raised the additional money required to pay off the balance. It took years of dedicated fundraising events, but we now have a headquarters signed, sealed and delivered.

Miriam proved to be not only an outstanding recruit but a dear and loyal friend. We shared a similar outlook on political philosophy, including a strong belief in a more balanced, two-party system. It formed the basis of a strong personal and political kinship. Her husband, Dr. Phil Hellreich, a successful dermatologist, also lent his support to the party and even took on the chairmanship of the Oahu County Committee. In 1996, he joined me in San Diego for the Republican National Convention, at which Senator Bob Dole from Kansas was nominated for president and former representative and Secretary of Housing and Urban Development Jack Kemp, from suburban Buffalo, New York, joined the ticket as the vice presidential nominee.[8]

The East-West Center

On October 14, 2003, I was appointed by Colin Powell, then U.S. secretary of state, to be a member of the board of governors of the East-West Center in Honolulu. I was honored to be asked because I knew of the Center's good work in educating and training future leaders, especially those in the Pacific nations.

The Center was established by the U.S. Congress in 1960 to bring together people from the United States, Asia and the Pacific in cooperative study, research and dialogue on areas of mutual concern.[9] It is an independent, public, nonprofit organization funded by the U.S. government and other member nations, as well as private and corporate donors.

I joined a prestigious group of people led by Charles Morrison, then president of the Center.[10] He was well known and respected by leaders of the Pacific nations and spearheaded many programs to enhance the political and economic conditions of those countries. He was assisted by local leaders including former governor George Ariyoshi and Victor Li , who served as president of the East-West Center from 1981 to 1989.[11] Outstanding and dedicated staff made the organization effective, including Nancy Lewis, director of research; Ricky Kubota, director of administration; and Terence Bigalke, director of education.

Those closest to Dr. Morrison on a daily basis were Pat Matsunaga, assistant to the president, and Carleen Gumapac, corporate secretary, who served effectively as the go-to person and conduit to the president.

Local fellow governors appointed by Governor Linda Lingle included Roland Lagareta, a construction company vice president,[12] and international development economist Puongpun Sananikone,[13] both of whom served as board chairman, as well as Miriam Hellreich; investment banker Ted Liu; his wife, attorney Betty Kwong Liu; hotelier Jean Rolles and successful small business executive and entrepreneur Eddie Flores.

After my four-year term was over, I was reappointed to the position by then secretary of state Condoleeza Rice. During my eight years on the board, meetings were held in the various participating areas, including Vietnam, Japan, and of course Washington, D.C., The meetings were attended by former East-West Center graduates who had become leaders in their countries. These contacts were, and still are, invaluable.

During my eight years on the board, one of our biggest challenges was ensuring adequate and stable federal funding for the East-West Center. The challenges were significant, but thanks to strong support from the Hawaii congressional delegation, in particular Senator Dan Inouye, as well as my extensive contacts among members of the Republican caucus on Capitol Hill, the East-West Center received appropriate funding during my years on the board. I also served as chair of the executive committee of the board during my tenure.

National Asian Pacific Center on Aging (NAPCA)

While in Congress, I had selected and been assigned to a subcommittee on aging as part of the Banking and Finance Committee. So, it was most appropriate that I would later be asked to become a member of the National Asian Pacific Center on Aging (NAPCA). This organization is dedicated to assisting aging citizens of Asian descent, particularly immigrant citizens who have difficulty with English language skills and limited knowledge of government programs available to assist them in finding jobs and programs.

William "Mo" Marumoto, managing director and partner of Global Executive Search, extended the invitation. Mo had 30 years of experience in both the private and public sectors. He was on the NAPCA board of directors and knew of my interest in the subject of aging.

I accepted in April 2005 and stayed on the board through March

2018, serving as chairman from 2011 to 2015, when a second member from Hawaii, Sylvia Yuen, PhD,[14] became a fellow director. During these years NAPCA was the nation's leading advocacy organization committed to the dignity and quality of life for Asian Americans and Pacific Islanders.[15] One outstanding NAPCA program that served our community well was the help line funded by the Department of Health and Human Services. This telephone bank was staffed by individuals who spoke many Asian languages, including Mandarin, Cantonese, Korean and Vietnamese. Their assistance helped elders interpret, understand and access the many available government programs and opportunities. The program was active in many cities across the country, including Seattle, San Francisco, Houston, Chicago, New York, Boston and Philadelphia, and was well received nationwide.

NAPCA's network of community-based organizations and the longtime support of the U.S. Department of Health and Human Services—plus the Department of Labor, the Environmental Protection Agency (EPA), the U.S. Department of Agriculture and numerous philanthropic organizations including Atlantic Philanthropies, the Walmart Foundation and the Estate of George Ujihara—improved the lives of many Asian elders.

Among many successful initiatives, the NAPCA Senior Community Service Employment Program (SCSEP) was especially effective. It was the only federally funded training program to help low-income unemployed adults age 55 and older prepare for future employment.

NAPCA's Senior Environmental Employment (SEE) program was created to help the EPA and other federal, state and local agencies meet environmental mandates while using the talents and experience of workers 55 years and older.

The Agriculture Conservation Experience Services program, funded by the U.S. Department of Agriculture, offers employment to experienced workers age 55 and over who provide technical support to the Natural Resources Conservation Service.

The experience of serving with this organization was most satisfying and I hope the good work we accomplished continues. All of the programs active during those years I served were instituted and coordinated by the outstanding talent of our then president and CEO, Christine Takada, and her able and dedicated staff.

Other positions I volunteered for included: member of the research committee for St. Francis Hospital in Honolulu; director, Straub Medical Research and Education Foundation, also in Honolulu; board of governors, Boys and Girls Club of Hawaii; director of the Hawaii Visitors Bureau; advisory council, American Red Cross, and senior advisory council of the Civil Air Patrol.

The Next Generation of Leaders

In 2017 I was introduced to the Center for Tomorrow's Leaders, an organization that is working to raise emerging leaders from among today's youth of all cultures and backgrounds. Betty Kwong Liu is an advisor to the organization and her children participated in CTL's programs as high school students. She introduced me to Katie Chang, the organization's executive director, and April Nakamura, its associate director.

Our first conversation was in Hilo, where I was to be honored by the Hilo High School Foundation. Earlier that day, we met for lunch with David Matsuura, a former legislator from Hilo. We reminisced about our legislative days, and our conversation quickly turned to new challenges facing our home. It became clear that Katie's work to inspire and empower the next generation is vital, particularly in our home community of Hilo.[16]

CTL programs focus on the concept that anyone can be a leader, and that leaders should come from every community. It's something I've been passionate about throughout my career. You don't have to be endowed—by name, background, status or financial standing—to be a leader. Leadership starts with the dream of a better outcome and the courage to speak up. Any student can take on this mantle.

CTL works with teachers and school administrators to identify public high school students with leadership potential, especially those in underserved communities. These students participate in a three-year leadership development course designed to expand their leadership capacity, create a platform for advocacy and raise their voices to effect educational reform. I love that these students work to improve their own schools or communities. Leadership starts with tackling local issues that affect you and doing something about it. With "small" wins comes the potential for bigger wins down the road.

From this school-based program, students can apply for the CTL Fellows program, a competitive program for juniors and seniors in high school. Every year, I get to engage with and mentor 20 of these promising, bright young people, who come from both public and private high schools.

The interaction is precious. It's wonderful to see students from very different schools and backgrounds come together. They are eager to learn, and shocked to hear about the world as it used to be—when women couldn't have credit cards in their own names, when there were no teachers' unions, when my husband and I couldn't buy a house because of our Japanese American heritage. They love the stories of my upbringing in Hilo, and my time as a teacher in Ohio, when I taught my students the hula. They laugh as I recount my interaction with President George H. W. Bush, telling him to "Stop bombing Kahoolawe!"

Liberal ideals often dominate our youth, and I think they're surprised to learn that conservative politicians also fight for a more equitable world.[17]

I share from my heart. I tell them anyone can be a leader. That coming from a small, rural community won't prevent you from thriving in Washington, D.C., That Hawaii, your home, needs you. That you shouldn't be afraid to think differently, and that you should always think deeply. That you should always have fun leading and remember that life is an adventure. That political rivals can be friends. And that I believe in you.

My Family

Participating in government as a state legislator and a member of

Congress were exciting years. And the satisfaction of contributing to my community in other ways was also stimulating and fulfilling. But of all of the work I've done, what brought me the most satisfaction was raising my family.

Each of my children found their way to productive, fulfilling lives, and success in their chosen fields.

My oldest son, Stanley Jr., who did outstanding and trusted service as my treasurer in the races for U.S. Senate and Hawaii governor, earned a degree in medicine and entered private practice as an internist. He later led research in the field of telemedicine, then in its infancy. Sadly, Stanley Jr., also inherited his father's heart condition. He died in October 2013, at the much-too-early age of 58.

My eldest daughter, Sandra, also completed her medical studies, married and became a practicing internist in Oregon. Margaret, the third child, also went into medicine, but preferred "patients who don't talk back." She graduated from veterinary school and started her practice in Los Gatos, California. She took a month away from her busy schedule to help with my gubernatorial campaign.

My fourth child, Stuart, was an outstanding tennis player, like his grandfather. After graduating from the University of Hawaii with a degree in computer science, he put his digital skills to use in my U.S. Senate and Hawaii governor campaigns. To this day, he continues to compete professionally as a nationally ranked senior player with other athletes in his age bracket.

My youngest, Laura, was in California at the time of the campaign for governor but returned home to help and continue her studies in computer science. She also has gone into the medical field, working in administration for Hawaii's Queen's Health Systems.

And I would be remiss if I didn't acknowledge the pleasure I felt from opportunities to treat my father to experiences that he wouldn't have dreamed of when he was working hard to provide for my mother, my sisters and me. He was thrilled when I took him to London to see *Cats* onstage. On a visit to the Grand Canyon, he rode a mule down the Bright Angel Trail, loving every minute of it.

And he felt like a VIP when he and my mother were treated to a first-class limo ride from the airport on the way to a wine-tasting trip to the Silverado Resort in Napa, which was then owned by Amfac. I was then a member of Amfac's board of directors, and my attendance was required at a board meeting held at the Silverado. I told my parents, "Why don't you come up? Join us! Take a trip into the Napa Valley wine country." I arranged the limo as a surprise.

Challenges Ahead

My father's impact on me can't be overstated. Above all else, I've tried to live by his core belief in the power of our collective will to bring about real and lasting change. That was a lesson he taught me when Hawaii was a far different place. In the world in which he raised us, it was all but unheard of that the daughter of a clerk would one day serve on his company's board of directors. Or that his daughter, who was denied housing because of her race just a few years after statehood, would 20 years later represent that state in the United States Congress.

My father, like many from immigrant families, took the long view. He taught us in his quiet, dignified way that there would be more defeats than victories, more disappointments than celebrations. But he never gave up. He never lost faith in our country, or in the promise implicit in the American dream that our children will reap the rewards if only we have the courage to fight for what's right.

I have tried my best to live up to my father's hopes and expectations. This book is a memoir of where I've succeeded, and where I've failed. I hear his voice even as I contemplate those failures. Winning, of course, is nice—and he took particular pride when my sisters and I won on the tennis court—but my father always taught us that the true measure of success comes in fighting with honor and courage, no matter what the final score.

In his last years, when his body began to fail him, I served as his primary caregiver. It was one of the most important roles I've played in the family. He and my late mother had sacrificed so much for their children. I was thankful that I had the opportunity to care for him at the end of his long life. He left us on December 27, 2002, surrounded by his family. He was 98.

Despite the years that have passed, I remember my father's words when I think of the many challenges that face a new generation in Hawaii. If there is one thing my career taught me, it's that leadership in public life is not a spectator sport. A leader can't be a leader without a corps of people who are willing to follow and get engaged in the public debate. More than ever, we need public leaders who can motivate others to act for the common good.

That's what I've tried to do in my public life in Hawaii, and in Washington, D.C., History will be the final judge of how successful I was over the years. What I do know without a doubt is that I gave it my all.

The Waialae Golf Club's "Fearless Foursome": Sylvia Tateishi, Althea Sato, Marion Sakurai and Pat.

Pat with one of the large Hawaiian quilts she sewed.

The board of governors of the East-West Center when Pat served:
Top row, left to right: Tai Young Lee, Richard Collins, Joan Bickson,
Daniel Berman, Albert Chang. Middle row, left to right: Lyn Flanigan,
Miriam Hellreich, Eddie Flores Jr. Pat Saiki, Puongpun Sananikone.
Bottom row, left to right: Charles Morrison, then president of the
East-West Center, Patricia Harrison and Roland Lagareta.

PART V ENDNOTES

1 "Both in 1981 and 1984 the band was one of four featured bands in the Pasadena Tournament of Roses Band Festival and marched in the world famous Tournament of Roses parade." https://www.kahukuhigh.org/apps/pages/index.jsp?uREC_ID=249435&-type=d&pREC_ID=574109

2 The school opened in January of 1961 as the Honolulu Day School at the Church of the Crossroads in Honolulu, providing educational services for young children diagnosed with what was then called "neurological dysfunction." In 1967 the school changed its name to Variety Club School for Learning Disabilities. In 1988 the school changed its name to Variety School of Hawaii. https://www.varietyschool.org/our-histoy [sic]

3 Carol McNamee: https://www.kitv.com/story/40007321/aging-well-madd-founder-carol-mcnamee-says-work-gives-her-pur-pose.

4 Initial licensure now requires a master's degree or its equivalent from an educational institution recognized by the board of the American Speech and Hearing Association, evidence of having met requirements for the ASHA Certificate of Clinical Competence, passage of a written exam and three letters of recommendation. https://www.asha.org/advocacy/state/info/HI/licensure/

5 Miriam Hellreich: https://ballotpedia.org/Miriam_Hellreich.

6 Linda Lingle was a former Maui County mayor, council member and chair of the Hawaii Republican Party. She was the first Republican governor in Hawaii in 40 years. https://ballotpedia.org/Linda_Lingle.

7 Duke Aiona served as Hawaii's tenth lieutenant governor from December 4, 2002, to December 6, 2010. He was the Republican nominee for governor in the 2010 election but was defeated by Democrat Neil Abercrombie in the general election. He ran again in 2014 but was defeated by Democrat David Ige. https://ballotpedia.org/Duke_Aiona.

8 1996 Republican National Convention: https://www.cnn.com/ALLPOLITICS/1996/conventions/san.diego/facts/delegate.profile/HI.shtml.

9 East-West Center: https://www.eastwestcenter.org/about-ewc/mission-and-organization.

10 "Charles E. Morrison has held several positions at the Center, including president from August 1, 1998 through December 30, 2016." https://www.eastwestcenter.org/about-ewc/directory/charles-e.morrison.

11 Charles Morrison: https://www.eastwestcenter.org/news-center/web-articles/former-ewc-president-victor-li-passes-away and https://www.staradvertiser.com/2013/09/20/breaking-news/victor-hao-li-former-east-west-center-president-dies/.

12 "Roland Lagareta, a construction company vice president, was Lingle's coordinator for the Nuuanu and Pali region..." http://archives.starbulletin.com/1999/05/24/news/story4.html.

13 Puongpun Sananikone: https://www.eastwestcenter.org/news-center/news-releases/ewc-board-elects-puongpun-sananikone-new-chairman.

14 Sylvia H. Yuen, PhD continued on the board until March 2019, when she was recognized as an exiting board member during a March 2019 NAPCA board meeting, according to the April 2019 "Advocacy with NAPCA" email newsletter.

15 Some of the others who served during Pat's tenure were David Cohen, who followed her as chair; David Kim, John Duong, Ruby Moy, Jack Chow, Anna Corssline, Yvonne Tatsuno and Deborah Ching.

16 CTL has offices in Hilo and Oahu, according to its website.

17 CTL Fellow Melissa Newsham: "Ms. Saiki is a legend in our state, especially for Republicans. She championed a set of alternative ideas in a predominantly Democratic state and worked with individuals on both sides of the aisle to get things done. She pointed out to us the dangers of the continued lack of political diversity in our state. During the interview, she encouraged us CTL students to speak up, both literally and figuratively. She reminded us that we must use our voice [sic] and share our ideas, and do so confidently. She, in many ways, represents a vibrant political culture which once existed in Hawaii."

Acknowledgments

My Japanese ancestors summarized the process of living life with humility and self-reflection in a word, *naikan*. I've thought of that word and what it means a lot during the writing of this book. Writing a book, I've discovered, is much like living a full life. You owe much to others, for their support and more. And one can never thank all who are deserving of thanks, let alone acknowledge one's debt of gratitude to all of those who made a difference.

The best I can do in these few paragraphs is to offer my thanks to a small group of friends and family who have helped me over the many, many months it took to turn a lifetime of memories into words on a page.

I would not be writing my political memoir if it wasn't for the early and loyal support from Raymond Torkildson, Roy King, James Napier, Dr. Franklin Kometani, Henry Walker Jr., Jack Magoon, Malcolm MacNaughton and from the thousands of people who volunteered for my campaigns and donated precious dollars that allowed me to run competitive races.

I must thank Miriam Hellreich and Betty Kwong Liu, who early on began urging me to "write your book." They gave me their own notes on what they remember of the many political battles we fought together as comrades in arms. They were persistent in reminding me to put myself in front of a keyboard and write. They have always given me candid, heartfelt advice. I trust them as if they were my sisters.

I must thank Mele Songsong and Karen Mau, two pros in their

own spheres, who provided invaluable help organizing dates, names, titles and much more.

I could not have completed the manuscript without their support. And special thanks to Debbie Minicola and the staff at Homelani Memorial Park in Hilo for their assistance.

I must thank Floyd K. Takeuchi and Karen Davis Barr, who helped me turn a rough manuscript into a compelling story. Floyd's been with me since 1987, when he accepted my invitation to serve on my congressional staff in Washington. He was known to most as my press secretary, but in reality, he did much more for me then, and over the many years since we worked together on Capitol Hill. Karen is a more recent member of my inner circle, but she's had an oversize influence on this memoir. I haven't met a more talented writer, editor and organizer than Karen. No surprise since she's a successful editor and publisher in her own right and has run her own publishing company for more than 30 years.

Thank you to George Engebretson, president and publisher of Watermark Publishing/Legacy Isle Publishing, who took a manuscript and turned it into a beautiful book.

And most of all, I must thank my children: my oldest, Stanley Saiki Jr., MD, who passed a few years ago, far too early; Sandra Williams, MD, Margaret Saiki, DVM, and Stuart Saiki, who live on the U.S. mainland but keep in close touch; and my youngest, Laura Saiki, who lives in Honolulu and has been my solid foundation for many years.

My sincerest gratitude to everyone who patiently and devotedly participated with me in the development of this document. Thank you so much.

—*Patricia F. Saiki*
Honolulu, Hawaii

Index